KINGDOM ESCHATOLOGY

THE GLORIOUS FUTURE
OF THE CHURCH

By Héctor P. Torres

Contributing Author: Ralph Woodrow

Published in Spanish By Editorial Peniel 2012
info@peniel.com o www.peniel.com
Buenos Aires, Argentina
54 11 4981-6178

Published in Portuguese by Publicacoes TRANSFORMA 2012
www.institutotransforma.org o contato@institutotransforma.org
Curitiba, PR Brazil
55 41 3095-2269

ISBN 978-958-737-099-7

Impreso en Colombia - Printed in Colombia

DEDICATION

I dedicate this book to my beloved wife Myriam. She has been my companion for over 40 years, my armor bearer, intercessor and ministry partner. She frequently tells me that when the enemy throws darts at me, I move and she gets hit by them. As of this writing, our daughters, grandchildren, family and friends are praying for her to receive a new heart, she is waiting for a heart transplant. Eighteen months ago doctors gave her six months to live BUT we have a God who is able to do exceeding abundantly above and beyond what we may ask or understand, a Savior who bore her sickness and promised her healing from all manners of sickness. We are looking through the eyes of faith and hope that he will give us the end that we desire.

Likewise, I dedicate this book to my granddaughter Maggie Hope Lent, whose miraculous life has been a demonstration of God's power, love and faithfulness to all our family and to His promises.

ENDORSEMENTS

The Dominion Mandate is one of strongest words that the Spirit is currently speaking to the churches. God expects us not only to save souls, but also to disciple whole nations. The history-makers of our generation will be transforming entire cities and regions for the kingdom of God, and our world will get better and better. The idea that some of us used to have that the church will be raptured and that Antichrist will take over, no longer can fit the serious implementation of the Dominion Mandate. How, then, should we think of the end times? Héctor Torres draws on his extensive historical knowledge, his skills in biblical exegesis, and his superb ability to communicate to give us important answers to that question in this book. I am excited about *Kingdom Eschatology*.

C. Peter Wagner, Apostolic Ambassador
Global Spheres, Inc.
President, Global Harvest Ministries
Founder and Chancellor Emeritus, Wagner Leadership Institute

Blessings,
C. Peter Wagner

Héctor Torres has had an extraordinary impact on Latin America. As a leader of many leaders, he is an apostle of the Holy Spirit for our generation. He is also deeply committed to a rich and full understanding of the Bible, so that he is well-qualified to deal with the important theological subjects in this book. Latin America is experiencing a massive revival and church growth, but the danger lies in the fact that leaders do not go deeper into their grasping of the Word of God and the Church history.

The ocean of revival can be miles wide, but it is not deeply rooted. My prayer is that this book will calm the stormy waters of the wrong theological interpretation and confusion, and will deepen the understanding of the Bible the Church has regarding the great theological subjects in Christian history.

Dr. Gary Kinnaman,
Author *Overcoming the Dominion of Darkness,*
And Signs Shall Follow, Angels Dark and Light and others.

To mention Hector Torres is to refer to one of the pioneers of the new apostolic reformation which, from the beginning of the spiritual warfare movements and intercession for the nations, Hector has led the Church to new spiritual dimensions in the Lord.

With *Kingdom Eschatology,* he introduces us into a new reading and analysis of history, which has a definite influence on the focus of the coming events. In this book, Hector Torres does not intend to repeat what others authors have already said and suggested. On the contrary, with great courage he dares to make a counter-proposition and, in a sense, to produce a counter-current. I am sure that the reader of this book will use it as permanent reference and consulting material due to its full and up-to-date contents.

The analytical approach, research and critical is excellently presented. And I tell you something, it removed some of my theological paradigms. But it makes so much sense to explain that, I wonder why we could not see the obvious!

This wonderful work will become a constant source to juggle the minds of those who are within reach of an erroneous theology inherited a new approach. On behalf of the Christian people all over the world, I say THANK YOU.

René Peñalba
International Christian Center, Tegucigalpa
Honduras, Central America.

Thank you Hector, for this new wonderful book. Your knowledge together with your biblical and historical perception are a treasure for the Church. I thank God for your tireless work to lead us to think about our mission in a creative way.

Throughout the centuries we have handed over our rights without God's authorization. Areas such as politics and arts, among others, are now under the control of the wicked. That is over! We are going to train and send the children of the People of God, as apostles of the Kingdom, to those areas. The Church is being empowered to transform, conquer and rule our nations. Not only we will continue to win souls, but also we will disciple our culture in order to bring it at the feet of our beloved Savior.

Congratulations Hector, on your ministry and this new and necessary literary work.

Dr. Alberto H. Mottesi, Evangelist
Author, *America 500 Years Later*
Alberto Mottesi Evangelistic Association

Yes! This is the "now word" that God's Spirit is heralding to the body of Christ around the world! Jesus gave us the great commission to "make disciples of the nations" and in Héctor Torres' timely and greatly inspired new book we have been given a powerfully clear and biblical teaching to release this truth into our lives. By a careful and comprehensive examination of the eight realms of culture and the kingdom of God's mandate, mission and wisdom for bringing transformation to these spheres of influence, *Kingdom Eschatology* gives us a powerful and practical roadmap for success. This is what God is saying and doing and

Héctor is the anointed, prophetic pioneer He has sent to herald this glorious truth!

Dr. Michael Maiden, Author *Turn the World Upside Down, God's Manifesto for the End Time Church, The Joshua Generation.*
Pastor of Church for the Nations
Phoenix, Arizona

This book will challenge you and hopefully change you! Hector Torres is not only a leader of many leaders in Latin America, but an apostle to all of us. With revival oftentimes comes wrong theological interpretation and confusion. Hector is in the unique position of both ushering in revival and also clarifying its foundational scriptural truths. He has a deep grasp of the Word of God, Church History and current practice; so that he is well-qualified to deal with the important theological subjects in this book. *Kingdom Eschatology* gives us a clear and practical understanding of end times truth. Leaders from all different streams of the Body of Christ would be wise to carefully study and embrace this book. A must read!

Alfred H Ells
Executive Director
Leaders that Last Ministries
Grace Association of Churches, Ministers and Ministries

This latest book of Hector Torres is a well researched and written work regarding the different teachings related to the end time church. It should be acknowledged that not everyone will agree with Hector's conclusions, however, his research will definitely stir your mind and your spirit to go back to the Word of God and search the Scriptures under the guidance of the Holy Spirit to hear with the Spirit is saying to the Church today. For

God has called us to bring transformation to every realm of society, and only a strong and victorious church can fully accomplish such a mandate. As you read, ask the Lord for revelation of His true at this critical hour in human history.

Dr. Naomi Dowdy
Founder of TCA College, Singapore
Apostle in God's Kingdom

I have said for years that, because of the prevalence of Dispensational Theology we need to have a theological transformation in the church before we will ever experience a societal transformation! Truly our eschatology will determine our protology. For this reason I applaud Dr. Hector Torres for his insightful contribution to this most important subject! As a world renowned apostle, teacher and intercessor, Dr. Torres's voice is needed more now than ever in Church if it is going to be equipped to function as salt and light once again in the world!

Bishop Joseph Mattera. Resurrection Church, Brooklyn N.Y.
Author *Kingdom Revolution, Kingdom Awakening, Ruling in the Gates*
Overseer Christ Covenant Coalition

PREFACE

N ever before has there been a greater concern and interest in the "end times". Maybe it is also appropriate to point out that never before has there been so much confusion and uncertainty about this issue. This is particularly true in Latin and North America, where both theories which are critically analyzed by the author of this book –Cessationism and Dispensationalism– are deeply rooted. The lack of a solid biblical, theological, historical and missiological foundation of these two speculative approaches has not prevented them from penetrating, especially in the evangelical realm, with its consequent negative effects.

Far from encouraging a healthy eschatological expectation of the glorious return of Christ, these convictions with their several variations have almost dissolved all hope and Christian practice. It is even worse the fact that, busy in drawing the many maps of the future, churches have lost their apostolic vocation. Unlike the early Christians, who were able to win the world for Christ in their generation, as a result of living a deep faith in the *imminent* and *future* coming of the Lord, many Christians today delay or put aside with indifference the fulfillment of the mission, in the belief that "there is plenty of time" Quite a few believers think that if this generation does not complete the mission, perhaps the next one or the one after will be able to do it. The early Christians did not think this way.

The author of this book helps us recover the apostolic way to understand the end times, and he does with faithful attachment to the biblical testimony. His effort to reinterpret more strictly some traditional conclusions among evangelicals is commendable. The reader may disagree with some details, but if the reading and studying of the next pages help him get rid of cessationist and dispensationalist ideas, the author's aim will be fulfilled.

In times like these, when the Holy Spirit is raising his gifts once again among believers; when Ephesians 4:11-12 is not just a hardly read and misunderstood passage but a real example of charismatic ministry for the training of all Christians for service; when there is a spread and deepened conviction that we have no much time left to complete the mission the Lord has entrusted to us, because He is at the door; when we are more aware than ever of our God-given power (Acts 1:8), and try to serve him in unity and not in dispersion or division, a book like the one written by Hector Torres becomes a proper encouragement for thought and action.

Pablo A. Deiros
Rector
International Theological Baptist Seminary
Buenos Aires, Argentina

PROLOGUE

The last decades have been marked, like never before in the Church history, by winds of change which have transformed the church environment. If we take time to think about the changes in praise and worship, programs of service, music and media of communication, new church finances and even the incursion of the Church into the Internet and social networks, all this leads us to admit that we are living in an age of important transitions, not only for the world and its globalization but also for Christianity. If we have experienced changes in every area, why should we not think that we need changes in the eschatological concepts that have prevailed in the Church for such a long time?

If eschatology as we know it were beneficial, we would surely not think of the necessity of new lines of eschatological thought; the fact is that this eschatology has been harmful because it has encouraged acceptance and fatalism. I remember that in my youth years, in the mid 60s and 70s, Christians wondered whether they should study and make progress when the "coming of our Lord Jesus Christ" was imminent; many lost interest in studying and others dropped out of school due to this kind of ideas.

Dispensationalism also fed fatalism through their outlook of a world under the control of the Antichrist, where the devil was the conqueror and God was was the loser; because He had to pick up a Church that had been unable and powerless to transform the world and take the gospel to the end of the Earth.

I believe we need books and documents with a new line of eschatological thought, and for that reason I would like to congratulate my good friend and fellow war-fighter, Apostle and Prophet Hector Torres on his courage to introduce new ideas which are necessary for the Church to adopt the line of thought of the Kingdom. We must "kill some sacred cows" in the eschatological field. New concepts usually face opposition, rejection, criticism and mockery; however, if it were for this, the Church would have never gone through a transition over the years. We are in need of new approaches. I am a professor and have taught biblical eschatology, that is why I am familiar with the different schools of thought as preterism, historicism and Dispensationalism, including idealism; however, in my opinion for a school of thought to fit the Bible and the current Church, it must spread the concepts of Kingdom and apostleship. I think *Kingdom Eschatology* is important not only due to its biblical investigative contents, but also due to the historical evaluation getting to the roots of Catholic Dispensationalism or futurism. We urgently need a new eschatology of the Kingdom to encourage the Church to take part in fields such as education, politics, arts, civil society, economy, science, technology, the media of communication and other areas of influence.

Since I was a child I have been hearing about the coming of our Lord Jesus Christ which I do not deny because it is an irreversible promise that our Savior has given us; however, futurism once and again has introduced facts, dates and characters about events that have not had their fulfillment. As someone once said: "Those who do not learn from history are condemned to repeat it". I think that Christ's words: *And this gospel of the kingdom will be preached in all the world as a witness to all the nations, and then the end will come (Matthew 24:14),* show that instead of accepting an escapist and fatalist eschatology we must pass from the gospel of salvation to the gospel of the Kingdom.

I strongly recommend this book *Kingdom Eschatology* because I believe it will open the understanding of many regular Bible readers and, at the same time, it will be a tool for sincere students of biblical theology who are expecting winds of change of the Kingdom and multiplication in the Church today.

Efraín Avelar
Genesis Christian University of Theology
Queltzaltenango, Guatemala
Central America Contents

CONTENTS

INSERT 1

INTRODUCTION

PART 1
KINGDOM ESCHATOLOGY AND DISPENSATIONALISM
Chapter 1: Kingdom Eschatology
Chapter 2: The Origen of Dispensationalism

INSERT 2

PART 2
JESUS' PROPHECIES
Chapter 3: Matthew 24 - Part 1
Chapter 4: Matthew 24 - Part 2
Chapter 5: The Great Tribulation

PART 3
THE PROPHECIES
Chapter 6: Daniel's Prophecy – The Little Horn, The Beast, 666
Chapter 7: Paul's Prophecy – The Man of Sin
Chapter 8: John's Prophecy – The Spirit of the Antichrist

PART 4.
THE COMING OF CHRIST
Chapter 9: Daniel's Seventy Weeks
Chapter 10: The Rapture or Catching up – Part 1
Chapter 11: The Rapture or Catching up – Part 2 The Millennium
Chapter 12: The One Hundred and Forty-four Thousand

PART 5
THE KINGDOM OF GOD AND THE KINGDOMS OF THIS WORLD
Chapter 13: Rediscovering the Principles of the Kingdom
Chapter 14: The Transformation of the Kingdoms of this World
Chapter 15: The Authority of the Kingdom

CONCLUSION

And so we have the prophetic word confirmed, which you do well to heed as a light that shines in a dark place, until the day dawns and the morning star rises in your hearts; knowing this first, that <u>no prophecy</u> of Scripture is of any <u>private</u> interpretation, for prophecy never came by the will of man, but holy men of God spoke as they were moved by the Holy Spirit.

2 Peter 1:19-21 (emphasis added by the author)

INTRODUCTION

I n the 1990's significant changes began to occur within
the Evangelical Church walls. More and more Church
leaders began to work together in order to fulfill the mandate
of the Great Commission and mobilize the Church worldwide
in prayer and intercession and a united vision for Community
Transformation. Many Church scholars began to refer to these
changes as *Post-Denominationalism.* Dr. C Peter Wagner referred
to these changes as the *"new apostolic reformation"*. Nowadays,
this movement is emerging all around the nations and cities of
the Christian world.

The Church walls are falling down and in the last few years
it has been experiencing a huge change: A shift from denominations and institutions to a vision and mission of the Kingdom
of God. As a part of that change, the old pastoral and leadership
alliances, as well as fellowships and councils are being replaced
by groups of leaders from different denominations and groups
of friendship and comraderhip, the foundation of which is their
personal relationships, a vision of the Kingdom of God and a
purpose of transformation in their communities.

Leaders with a territorial vision for their cities and regions are
coming together, despite their doctrinal differences. Their heart
is to bring transformation into their communities in the spiritual
realm, an awakening in the spirit, a visitation from God, but
above all, a church "reformation" based on the restoration of
the ministry of apostles and prophets as the foundation of the

Church (Ephesians 2.20). To bring a restoration of the lost truths distorted by traditions and false teachings and philosophies which are contrary to the sound doctrine received from the Church fathers.

The first question we should ask ourselves is: What is a reformer? The word is used to describe those people who wish to come back to the foundations of the Word of God and the original truth of the gospel. As my friend Al Ells states: "someone who has a divine vision and revelation of God's truth for this season in a sphere of kingdom influence"

Wrong doctrines have crept into the Church due to the corruption and contamination of human traditions and the apostasy of the Church. A reformer's intentions, analyzed from the point of view of Church history, stood out especially in the reformation of the fallen Roman Catholic Church.

To reform something is to correct what is incorrect or to rectify, repair or change something. God has always sent reformers to bring the necessary changes to His people and His Church, so that it may be able to rise to new levels.

Christ began the reformation in the transition of the covenant of the law to the covenant of grace. Through Jesus Christ, God's economy had a radical change. The new covenant established by the death of Christ makes those who are called; receive the promise of the eternal inheritance. Jesus Christ introduced a reformation into the ministry order, which He identified as apostles. A parallel ministry to that of the judges in the Old Testament and which, by human ordinances, had been lost in the government of the people of Israel.

When God wants to introduce changes, He raises reformers and imparts an apostolic anointing to them. They are sent to reform or restore all that religion, tradition or the conquest forced over the people of God. Reformers are raised by God to break all that man and religion have imposed on them, as well as to restore the truths which have been lost due to the same reason.

The apostle has the authority and the anointing to break all that tradition and religion have brought upon us and let us step into the changes of God. God restores abundantly what the enemy has stolen. For this, we need an apostolic grace that will let us break through and change the old patterns. It is a pioneering work that reaches to enter into unknown places.

The reformation or restoration also brings "revelation". Historical reformers gradually received revelation of the teachings that the Church had lost due to the corruption of the Roman Catholic Church. God continues to bring reforms into his Church. The expression *semper reformada* should be a constant practice in our Christian faith. In the Church, God is always reforming and restoring his truths until we reach the restoration of all things declared by the Lord.

Jesus Christ was establishing a new order that he called "new wineskins". When we get accustomed to things, we enter a comfort zone that produces great opposition toward the arrival of something new.

In Matthew 5:6-7 we read the words of a "sent one", a reformer. The apostle brings a redefinition of concepts which are different from the ones taught and learned in the past, Jesus Christ gave his authority to the disciples for them to make disciples of all nations, teaching them to keep everything He has commanded them. When an apostle brings new revelation to the Church, many do not understand it and he becomes a pioneer bringing "new wine". Many times the old wineskins are our own prejudices, thoughts and doctrines. Often, the reaction to the apostolic pioneers is negative because they come to challenge Christians' current way of thinking. The opposition usually comes from those who are challenged or confronted with their own errors.

In the Sermon on the Mount, the Lord redefined the doctrines and teachings of the Pharisees. You have been told... but "I tell you"...; you have heard... but "I tell you"... He literally brought a revelation of the lost truths. The Pharisees knew the letter, but not the Spirit of the Word. Here, once and again, the doctrines of the past, and the teachings of former generations are challenged. Jesus Christ, like every reformer, challenges those beliefs and corrects the concepts with fresh revelation directly from the Word of God. The accusations of the Pharisees about Christ are exactly these: *Then the high priest tore his clothes, saying, "He has spoken blasphemy! What further need do we have of witnesses? Look, now you have heard His blasphemy! What do you think?"* They answered and said, "He is deserving of death." (Mathew 26.65-66) The contradictions to their doctrines led them to the point of demanding his death.

When God began to reveal his truths after the falling away prophesized by Apostle Paul, all the reformers were accused as heretics and many of them were killed. The future generations need to know about the heroes of the past. The martyrs of the early Church such as Polycarp, Ignatius and Justin, patriarchs of the Church; in the Middle Ages, men and women as John Wycliffe, John Huss and Joan of Arc; during the Renaissance William Tyndale, Martin Luther, John Calvin, Huldrych Zwingli and Theodore Beza, are only some of the reformers who were accused of heresy by the religious institutions. The Book of Martyrs by John Fox has a detailed account of the persecutions of Christians considered heretics.

Martin Luther was excommunicated and ordered to recant his written words, otherwise he would be judged as a heretic by the emperor and the leaders of the Roman Church; but he refused to do it and said: "Unless you can convince me by Scriptures or by clear reasoning, I will not accept the authority of the pope and the councils who have contradicted each other. My conscience is captive to the Word of God. I cannot and I will not recant because to go against my conscience is neither right nor good. God help me. Amen."

Author Cindy Jacobs wrote: "Today, like in the days of Huss, Luther and the Moravians, God is calling the believers of all generations to arise, listen to what the Holy Spirit is saying and adjust our religious structures with no fear of persecution. There is often a tendency to resist the new things that God wishes to do in order to keep our traditions, although they do not match the Bible. Others want to keep their positions of control and power in the body of the Church instead of letting God do his work. They choose their religious dogmas and legalism instead of letting God touch lives and transform communities." [1]

Over the years, the religious institutions that were supposed to defend the lost truths became the accusers. When Charles Finney started to minister all around New England and thousands of people accepted Jesus during the revival that preceded him, the Christian leaders from those regions accused him as a heretic because he had had the courage to call himself an evangelist and this ministry, according to them, did not exist any longer.

---

1   C. Jacobs, The Reformation Manifesto, Bethany House Publishers, 2008, p.59

The Pentecostal movements of faith and prosperity, renewal, spiritual warfare, the apostolic and prophetic restoration, territorial transformation and others that over time became a part of the teachings of the Church always faced opposition and were considered doctrinal heresy.

We are entering new challenges: the Kingdom of God and his Dominion and ruling over nations and human cultures, triumphant eschatology, the new Earth, the eternal dwelling place of the saints, the New Jerusalem and many other things that will be the subject-matter of the next theological debates.

Vishal Mangalwadi, one of the contemporary reformers, author of *"Truth and Transformation"*, called by the renowned Christian magazine Christianity Today the most important Christian intellectual in India, the author of thirteen books and an international lecturer, recently said: "We won't be able to have a worldwide 'transformation' if first we don't reeducate the Church about the errors of Dispensationalism and we teach the eschatological truths of the Word of God."

The Protestant Reformation reaffirmed the victorious and glorious contents of the biblical truth. This can be summarized in the following five expressions that characterized it:

Sola Christus (through Christ alone)

Sola Scriptura (by Scripture alone)

Sola gratia (by grace alone)

Sola fide (by faith alone)

Sola Deo gloria (glory to God alone)

This book is not a new revelation; *Kingdom Eschatology* is a compilation of the beliefs of the apostles, patriarchs and reformers based on the doctrinal roots of the Church throughout its history. As people called to bring reforms, we must remember all those who, at a high price, paved the way to restore truths that today we have as the biblical foundations by which we live.

It is our wish, that by the reading of this book of an apostolic, prophetic and apologetic nature, you will be challenged to study diligently the wonderful truths of the Word of God; and that this may lead the Church to a change of patterns in its calling to a vision of Kingdom, and provide a challenge for a final "reformation". Revival brings changes into a weak and dead Church; the spiritual awakening brings new believers to the Church, but reformation puts men and women of God in every area of influence in society and cultures to bring transformation and promote the Kingdom of God.

Everything that has happened, is now happening or will happen in the future is the result of the choices made by others or by ourselves. From the beginning of creation God gave mankind the ability to direct their destiny through the choices they made. We can choose life or death, blessings or curses.

God has revealed to us through His Word His manifold wisdom, his will, for His creation and His Ekklesia. Unless we have a clear understanding of His plans and purposes for the Church, we will not be able to lead God's people towards the fulfillment of their calling; that is why we must understand the Glorious Future of the Church. This is possibly the most important reason for a correct perspective of Kingdom Eschatology.

How we view the future determines what we do today to prepare the following generations. What we do today determines what will happen tomorrow.

Héctor Torres

PART 1

KINGDOM ESCHATOLOGY AND DISPENSATIONALISM

CHAPTER
1

KINGDOM
ESCHATOLOGY

*epent therefore and be converted, that
your sins may be blotted out, so that
times of refreshing may come from the presence
of the Lord, and that He may send Jesus Christ,
who was preached to you before, whom heaven
must receive until the times of restoration of all
things, which God has spoken by the mouth of
all His holy prophets since the world began.—
Acts 3:19-21*

BACK TO THE SOURCE

The doctrines, traditions and paradigms we have inherited
from religion, society or culture resemble a distorted mirror that
stops us from seeing the light or receiving revelation; likewise,
the voices of those people who have had a profound impact on
our minds through their work, actions and teachings.

On February 2, 1976, I became a Christian and accepted Jesus Christ as my Lord and Savior. Since that encounter with Jesus Christ I became a passionate student of the Word of God. Just a few days after this wonderful experience, I bought different versions of the Bible, several Old and New Testament study guides, W.E. Vine M.A.'s *Expository Dictionary of New Testament Words,* the *Essential writings* by Josephus, and every available book or reading material to help me go deeper in the knowledge of the Scriptures. The apostle Paul's advice to Timothy was the first Bible verse which was revealed to me as God's *rhema:* a living, practical message for my life:

> ***Be diligent to present yourself approved to God, a worker who does not need to be ashamed, rightly dividing the word of truth. 2 Timothy 2:15***
>
> ***... correctly handles the word of truth... (NIV)***
>
> ***... knows how to use the word of truth to the best advantage... (J. B. Phillips New Testament)***

Since then, those words from Scripture have been the solid foundation for the ministry the Lord has called me to do. The following passages are an encouragement for us to pay careful attention to the Word of God and above all, to the prophecies we can find throughout its pages. In order to be able to understand and retain our spiritual fathers' teachings, we should do our best to study the Bible as well as the writings of the Church patriarchs and reformers.

And so we have the prophetic word confirmed which you do well to heed as a light that shines in a dark place, until the day dawns and the morning star rises in your hearts; knowing this first, that no prophecy of Scripture is of any private interpretation, for prophecy never came by the will of man, but holy men of God spoke as they were moved by the Holy Spirit. 2 Peter 1:19-21

> *The word of prophecy was fulfilled in our hearing! You should give that word your closest attention, for it shines like a lamp amidst all the dirt and darkness of the world, until the day dawns, and the morning star rises in your hearts. But you must understand this at the outset that no prophecy of scripture arose from an individual's interpretation of the truth. 2 Peter 1:19-20, (J. B. Phillips New Testament)*

> *Above all, you must understand that no prophecy of Scripture came about by the prophet's own interpretation of things. 2 Peter 1:20, (NIV)*

By reading these passages we can conclude that they are referring to the Word of God as a whole and particularly, to the prophecies received from Him. Therefore, it is in the Scriptures where we will certainly be able to find God's will for our lives.

> *But as for you, speak the things which are proper for sound doctrine. Titus 2:1*

> *And they continued steadfastly in the apostles' doctrine... Acts 2:42*

> *For the time will come when they will not endure sound doctrine, but according to their own desires, because they have itching ears, they will*

heap up for themselves teachers; and they will turn their ears away from the truth, and be turned aside to fables. 2 Timothy 4:3

For the time is coming when men will not tolerate wholesome teaching. They will want something to tickle their own fancies, and they will collect teachers who will pander to their own desires. They will no longer listen to the truth, but will wander off after man-made fictions. (J. B. Phillips New Testament)

For the time will come when people will not put up with sound doctrine. Instead, to suit their own desires, they will gather around them a great number of teachers to say what their itching ears want to hear. (NIV)

...children, tossed to and fro and carried about with every wind of doctrine... Ephesians 4:14

These specific verses, among many others, led me not only to the reading of the Word of God but also to a careful study of it. In the same way I felt obligated to question any teaching which could be contrary to the Holy Scriptures. Regardless of the Word's messenger or teacher I developed the habit of double-checking everything I learned. On the other hand, I started to notice the fact that every preacher or teacher in church had a personal interpretation or opinion of the same Bible passages, especially those in the realm of eschatology and the prophetic.

Throughout the years I have been challenged by many people to study in depth all the different subjects that are taught in the Church today some of which are difficult to understand. One of those people has been my friend and fellow minister for more than thirty years: Ralph Woodrow, the author of several books such as *Babylon Mystery Religion, Great Prophecies of the Bible, His Truth is Marching On!* among other bestsellers. I must also mention other important Bible teachers such as my spiritual father Jack Hayford from the U.S.A, Pablo Deiros from Argentina, René Peñalba from Honduras, Apostle Efraín Avelar from Guatemala, C. Peter Wagner from the U.S.A, the Pastor of Presidents: Alberto Mottesi, Andrew Wommack from the U.S.A and my pastor and friend of over 30 years Dr. Gary Kinnaman.

THE TRUTH OR THE END OF THE WORLD? IS THE END COMING?

Eschatology, or the study of the end times, is one of the subjects that has given rise to the highest number of opinions in the Church today. In my opinion, the more the apostolic ministry looks to the beliefs of the original apostles, known as *sound doctrine*, the more these theories will be transformed. It is only through the careful study of the patriarchs' messages to the Church, the inheritance of their writings and the Protestant reformers' eschatological concepts, that we will eventually be able to understand that Christians have been misled into false teachings.

The apostolic calling is to restore these truths to the Church.

These truths have been hidden but God is gradually revealing them so that the Church may reach a final state of maturity, which will let it fulfill the precious and challenging calling to subdue and have dominion over all of God's creation and to establish his eternal Kingdom.

I firmly believe that the greatest danger for the future of the Church is what is currently known as Dispensationalism or futurism; a particular school of thought and interpretation of the last days.

There are three main schools of thought, or rather, three different "interpretations" of the Bible:

1. *The preterist interpretation or preterism:* According to this, all the acts described in Daniel, Mathew 24 and Revelation refer to events which took place during the first two centuries of the Church. It is also known as *idealism.*

2. *The historicist interpretation:* It sees the prophecies as a part of the historical process of all the events throughout history. The views and writings of the Early Church, the Church Patriarchs and the Protestant Reformers.

3. *The futurist or dispensationalist interpretation:* It contends that there is a lost week, for some people two different periods of three years and a half, and another one of seven years called the "great tribulation" which begins with the appearance of a man known by the title of the Antichrist and includes a particular view of the rapture and the presence of 144,000 Jews, 12,000 from each tribe, all virgins; who over a short period of time will be able to do without the aid of the Holy Spirit what the Church has not been able to carry out for more than 2,000 years *with* the manifestations and the power of the Holy Spirit.

The Church's health, as well as an apostolic perspective have been greatly affected by this type of interpretations. What kind of a church is God building up? What kind of a church has been called to place its enemies under its feet? What kind of church will Christ gather at His second coming?

Human ideas turned into beliefs and teachings eventually become philosophical strongholds. In my opinion, Dispensationalism is presently the most powerful philosophical stronghold in the Church.

Among the teachings of Dispensationalism, these are the most serious dangers for the Church:

1. *Escapism:* it is the rapture of Christians to heaven so that they may be able to avoid the coming judgment at the hands of a man called the Antichrist.

2. *Fatalism:* a defeated, powerless Christian Church which renounces God's calling to conquer cities, nations, regions and kingdoms for Christ.

3. *Humanism:* man has the answer for everything and applies any necessary methods; this is the principle behind the liberation theology.

"After the horrors of the American civil war, the eschatological perception turned into hiper-dispensationalism, an approach to Premillennialism, a belief that will not give place to a victorious Church bringing in permanent, positive changes in society but witnessing a decaying situation in the world as well as the Church. The outcome of this idea is an inept Church which must be taken to heaven before the Antichrist takes over the world; after that the second coming of Jesus will take place. Instead of sharing the possibility of change in society, a great emphasis is given to the prevailing of the power of Satan and sin with the only hope of being taken away for the Church."[2]

---

2   Joseph Mattera. Ruling in the Gates, Creation House Press

The Church of today is suffering from a serious disorder, like a disease that we could name *"theological schizophrenia"*. We believe what we doubt and we doubt what we believe. Our beliefs have been contaminated by Catholicism. Many of our beliefs have their origin in Roman Catholic Church doctrines and traditions. *An analysis of the biblical teaching about the second coming of Christ, the millennium, the kingdom of God, the nature and purpose of the Church, the Kingdom prophecies, etc. demonstrates that the teachings of Dispensationalism are theologically and exegetically inconsistent with the Word of God.*[3]

The apostle Paul warns us about the deception that comes into the Church by philosophies and traditions: ***"See to it that no one takes you captive through philosophy and empty deception, according to the tradition of men, according to the elementary principles of the world, rather than according to Christ." Colossians 2.8***

Let us have a look at the most popular teaching which is largely believed by Christians today, particularly in the Charismatic Pentecostal Church. The Church has lost sight of its mission, calling and purpose due to the lack of knowledge of the Bible truth which not only deprives us of life, but also makes us slaves.

The term eschatology means the study of the end times, death, resurrection, judgment and eternal life.

The Catholic Church considers eschatology as the study of life after death therefore ignoring the divine calling of the Church for the future.

---

3   The Premillenial Illusion. Brian Schwertly. Portuguese edition.

Acts 3:18 speaks about times of refreshing and times of restoration.

But those things which God foretold by the mouth of all His prophets, that the Christ would suffer, He has thus fulfilled. Repent therefore and be converted, that your sins may be blotted out, so that <u>times of refreshing</u> may come from the presence of the Lord, and that He may send Jesus Christ, who was preached to you before, whom heaven must receive until the <u>times of restoration of all things</u>, which God has spoken by the mouth of all His holy prophets since the world began. Acts 3:18-21 (emphasis added by the author)

The times of refreshing started on the day of Pentecost and represent the promise of relief and comfort for every Christian's life.

The times of restoration refer to the fulfillment of God's plan for his creation, of those things which were lost in the Garden of Eden and those declared by God's Word

---

A ruling people that have dominion bear fruit and are multiplied.

It is a people that establish God's Kingdom here on earth, as in heaven. A people who exercise dominion as it transforms cities and nations to the obedience of Christ.

The Bible teaches us that Jesus will remain in heaven until the fulfillment of God's words spoken through his holy prophets. That is, until we have placed his enemies under his feet. This is the condition: the good news of the Kingdom of God is preached in every nation and his enemies are defeated.

For the LORD Most High is awesome; He is a great King over all the earth. He will subdue the peoples under us, and the nations under our feet... For God is the King of all the earth; sing praises with understanding. Psalm 47:2-3, 7 (emphasis added by the author)

The LORD said to my Lord: "sit at My right hand, till I make Your enemies Your footstool". Psalm 110:1

Mathew 22:44, Mark 12:36, Luke 20: 42-43 and Acts 2:34-35 mention this passage and explain that Jesus will continue to be seated at the right hand of his Father; He will not return *until* his enemies are put under his feet.

But this Man, after He had offered one sacrifice for sins forever, sat down at the right hand of God, from that time waiting till His enemies are made His footstool. Hebrews 10: 12-13

Then comes the end, when He delivers the kingdom to God the Father, when He puts an end to all rule and all authority and power. For He must reign till He has put all enemies under His feet. 1 Corinthians 15:24-25

And the God of peace will crush Satan under your feet shortly. The grace of our Lord Jesus Christ be with you. Romans 16:20

In Romans 16:20, Paul's announces Christ and his Church's final victory over evil, as the fulfillment of Genesis 3:15. "Shortly" does not mean "soon", but "quickly". We can be sure that the Lord's victory over Satan's deeds will be overwhelming at the end of the present world.

Will crush, *suntribo; Strong #4937: Knock down, break, destroy, crush, grind, quash. The expression in verse 20 refers to Genesis 3:15. Our victory is an extension of Christ's victory, when He bruised the head of the serpent on the cross of Calvary. Suntribo suggests not only the current victories over the powers of darkness, but also the final destruction of Satan's kingdom on the second return of Jesus.*[4]

REMOVING THE VEIL

The greatest enemies of restoration are:

- *Cessationism:* the belief that God's power manifestations ceased together with the completion of the New Testament. Today there are no apostles or prophets, and miracles such as healings and other gifts of the Holy Spirit do not occur any longer. Most of these doctrines belong to the historic churches. *Abundant teaching with little power.*

- *Dispensationalism:* we will analyze its origin and teachings in a later chapter, but we can define it as the dispensations of the end times, also known as *futurism.*

What we know today as "The Reformation" was the beginning of the restoration of the teachings of the early Church which had been lost, removed or forgotten over time; these are the biblical truths restored throughout the years:

       a. Salvation

       b. Baptism

       c. Holiness

       d. Missions

       e. The Baptism with the Holy Spirit

---

4   Hayford, Jack W., General Editor, Spirit Filled, (Nashville, TN: Editorial Caribe) 2000, c1994.

f. The spiritual gifts for the ministry, abilities, etc.

g. Worship

h. Finances

i. Church Government

j. Leadership

k. Spiritual warfare

l. Five-fold ministry

m. Apostleship and Spiritual paternity.

n. The Kingdom of God

o. God's truth (the logos is an expression of God's will)

The Church is a body of authority, dominion, power and kingdom.

The teachings of Dispensationalism are totally contrary to an apostolic theology, and even to a theology of kingdom and dominion.

Paul, John and Peter's teachings are a theology of victory, conquest, triumph, power and influence.

...and what is the exceeding greatness of His power toward us who believe, according to the working of His mighty power which He worked in Christ when He raised Him from the dead and seated Him at His right hand in the heavenly places, far above all principality and power and might and dominion, and every name that is named, not only in this age but also in that which is to come. And He put all things under His feet,

and gave Him to behead over all things to the church, which is His body, the fullness of Him who fills all in all. Ephesians 1:19-23

Now to Him who is able to do exceedingly abundantly above all that we ask or think, according to the power that works in us... Ephesians 3:20

In 2 Corinthians 10:4, Paul explains that our God-given weapons have the power to demolish any kind of strongholds of our enemies. The Bible says that no weapon of the devil can do us harm (Ephesians 6:16, John 2:13-14, 1 John 5:18). If God is with us, who can be against us? He who is within us is greater or more powerful than the one who is in the world.

...to an inheritance incorruptible and undefiled and that does not fade away, reserved in heaven for you, who are kept by the power of God through faith for salvation ready to be revealed in the last time. 1 Peter 1:4-5

Paul declares that the Kingdom of God is not a matter of words but of power (1 Corinthians 4:20); and we read in Colossians 1:11 that we are strengthened in our inner being by the power of his glory.

All these scriptures, and many others, describe a Church with the calling to bring Christ's lordship into lives, to transform nations and to establish his Kingdom on earth so that we will be able to give it back to Him on his second coming. Jesus will not return for a Church which is seduced by the world and its powers, a Church which expects Him to fulfill its own mission. He will return for a glorious Church, without stain or wrinkle, that honors his name. And above all, a Church that has made his enemies his footstool.

In Ephesians 2:1-3 and 1 John 5:29 we read that this world receives the influence and is under the control of our enemy and evil; but the Bible never says that Satan has the right to keep the present situation just the way it is. On the contrary, it is to establish God's will on Earth as it is in Heaven.

Triumphant eschatology establishes God's seasons and times (<u>kairos</u>). The Church will not be transformed until it clearly understands the Kingdom of God and the Ekklesia's glorious calling.

We are still writing the history of the Church. God's calling for us is not to hear or read about history, but to take part in it. We are a generation chosen by the Lord to live days like these ones. The 21st century Church has the opportunity to produce the greatest reform since the beginnings of Christianity. The only way that can happen requires the re-education of God's people and the raising of a new generation of reformers that have a Kingdom vision and perspective.

CHAPTER
2

THE ORIGIN OF DISPENSATIONALISM

But there were also false prophets among the people, even as there will be false teachers among you, who will secretly bring in destructive heresies, even denying the Lord who bought them, and bring on themselves swift destruction. And many will follow their destructive ways, because of whom the way of truth will be blasphemed.—2 Peter 2:1-2

DESCRIPTION OF DISPENSATIONALISM

Dispensationalism or futurism, as it is better known, began after the Protestant Reformation in 1517. As we will see, it originated as part of the Catholic Church's "**Counter Reformation**".

The book of Revelation became a weapon of war which cost millions of lives for almost two centuries.

During the third century there were a number of problems regarding the interpretation of the book of Revelation. Clement of Alexandria (150-215 A.D.) and Origen of Alexandria (185-254 A.D.), two of the most renowned theologians at that time, taught that this book was a symbol of the fight between good and evil, the kingdom of God and the kingdom of darkness; but it did not refer to future events at all. This became known as *idealism*. Some of the early Church patriarchs, such as Dionysius of Alexandria, denied its authenticity. Irenaeus, Bishop of Lyon, confirmed that the book was authentic being himself a disciple of Policarp, who was a disciple of Apostle John.

The Protestant Reformation was strengthened on the basis of three basic truths:

1. The Bible is the Word of God and has priority over tradition and the laws of the Catholic Church. *"Sola Scriptura"*.

2. Salvation can only be obtained through Christ. This is by grace and through faith. *"Sola Gratia"*.

3. The papacy is the Antichrist and Rome is the harlot of Babylon.

The reformers unanimously and bravely accepted these truths as holy and, with the guidance of their own conscience, took a strong stand against the papacy as the Antichrist and the Roman Catholic Church as the harlot of Babylon. This act produced a schism in the Christian world which almost destroyed the papacy.

A journey back to the time of the Protestant Reformation takes us to the beginning of the truth of this interpretation. During this period of the Church, the common understanding of the fulfillment of these prophecies was attacked in its interpretation and totally distorted. The resulting confusion from this theological attack remains to the present day. This can be seen in the teaching of a seven-year period of tribulation, called *the great tribulation*, which will take place in the future. This idea was born in opposition to the reformation in the 16th century.

As a consequence, the reformation was followed by a Catholic counter-reformation which included five main points:

1. The recognition of the Society of Jesus (Jesuits).

2. The Council of Trent and its official decrees, such as:

    •   The prohibition of Bible reading or possession.

    •   The declaration of Protestants as heretics.

3. A Catholic system of prophetic interpretation.

4. The faith index (the dogmas of the Roman Catholic faith).

5. A persecution of the *heretics* as the new believers were called, also known as "The Medieval Inquisition"

In their letters, Paul, Peter and John refer to these men that gave birth to such teachings and made additions to them over the years, as false prophets, apostles and teachers. Today, many people continue to teach these things due to their lack of knowledge which proves what Jesus said that even the chosen ones would be deceived.

False prophets and false doctrines...Danger!

In 1590 Jesuit Francisco Ribera published a 500-page commentary on the books of Daniel and Revelation. At the same time, another Jesuit called Robert Bellarmine widened Ribera's interpretation which basically became known as Dispensationalism or futurism with the title of *Controversial teachings of discussed points over Christian beliefs against contemporary heretics*. Le Roy Edwin Froom writes: *Ribera assigned the first three chapters of Revelation to ancient Rome and the rest, 3 ½ years, to the kingdom of an unfaithful man: the Antichrist, who would oppose the saints before Christ's second coming. He would rebuild the temple of Jerusalem, suppress Christian religion, deny Christ, be welcomed by the Jews, pretend to be God and conquer the world.*[1]

In 1614 a Jesuit from Seville, by the name of Luis de Alcazar, introduced a preterist commentary with the title of *An investigation of the hidden meaning of Revelation;* his interpretation was that the prophecies of the Antichrist and Revelation had been fulfilled with the early Church, the destruction of Jerusalem and the fall of the Roman empire in 410 A.D.

Ribera' theory remained literally lost until Manuel Lacunza, a Chilean Jesuit (1731-1801), wrote two volumes with the title of *The coming of the Messiah in glory and majesty.* Lacunza's main teaching was that the return of Christ would happen in two different moments; in the first part the Church would be *raptured* so that it would be able to escape from the kingdom of the future Antichrist and the great tribulation in the hands of the man of sin.

---

1   L. E. Froom. The prophetic faith of our fathers, Vol. II, 484-505, The Review and Herald
     Publishing Assn. Wash. DC, 1948

In 1827 Edward Irving translated this work into English. Irving had no idea that Lacunza, who in his writings presented himself as *Josafat Ben Ezra*, was a Jesuit priest and not a converted Jewish rabbi, as he pretended to be. Under complete deception, Irving rejected the traditional teachings of Christianity.

Ribera denied the position of the Protestant Reformation on the Antichrist (the man of sin in 2 Tes. 2:2) as seated in the temple of God and held by Augustus, Jerome, Luther and many other reformers replacing him with an unfaithful Antichrist from outside the Church.[2]

The result of Ribera's work was the falsification and defamation of the prophetic truth.[3]

Edward Irving's prophetic point of view was mostly based on the theories of Jesuit authors and on his friend Samuel T Coleridge's ideas; they are apparently the foundation of Irving's millennarist teaching.

A mixture of Irving and Coleridge's opinions were probably focused on the mythical and dark aspect and gave birth to the doctrine of millennarism...it was through Irving that Lacunza's theories were introduced to the leaders of the Plymouth Brethren, such as John Nelson Darby, who attended the famous Powerscourt Conferences on Bible prophecy (1826-30) in Albury Park —the home of Lady Powerscourt— in Dublin, Ireland and other places between 1830 and 1840.

His book "The humanity of Jesus Christ" caused great offence in the Church of Scotland; in 1832 Irving was dismissed and excommunicated from the Church for heresy due to his obsession with prophecy and the alleged abuse of the Holy Spirit's manifestations. In

2   R. Thompson. Champions of Christianity in search of truth. P.89
3   R. Caringol. Seventy weeks: The historical alternative.P.32

1833 he founded his own church, the Holy Catholic and Apostolic Church. Irving died the following year.[4]

John Nelson Darby brought the Jesuit teachings into the reformed Church. Darby, famous for being the founder of the *Plymouth Brethren*, was an Anglican and attended the Power-scourt Conferences where he heard the idea of a *secret rapture* in two stages. He brought those ideas into the Plymouth Brethren and they soon reached the very heart of Protestantism. Later on, his teachings became popular in the reference notes of the Sco-field Bible.

Darby was influenced by Irving and supported by Cyrus I. Scofield, and the three of them were known as the first dispensationalists; Lewis S. Schafer and Charles Ryrie followed them and established that the pre tribulation was normative eschatology which became the basis of pre millennialism. Its main and central theory deals with the fact that Jesus Christ will return on a secret coming, called the *rapture,* in which Christian believers will be caught up during the *tribulation* period; after seven years, or three years and a half (according to a different interpretation), He will come back with them to defeat the Antichrist and his forces and establish God's millennial Kingdom on earth. Darby's teaching was known as *Precious truths revived.*

In 1834 Joseph Wolff, a former Catholic priest who was Darby's assistant, travelled throughout Ireland and Great Britain in representation of the London Bible Society, but sharing Darby's teachings. Wolff had a close friendship with Bishop John Henry Newman and Charles Butler, a prominent Catholic lawyer, and many others, which helps us understand why Darby accepted the Roman Catholic teachings and literature so easily.

---

4   F. F. Bruce, The Humanity of Jesus Christ, Journal of the Christian Brethren. 1973

Darby travelled to America several times and it was there, in Dr. Brooks' Presbyterian Church that he met Cyrus Scofield, one of Brook's students; later on Scofield published Darby's teachings and his notes in his Bible version (Scofield). The prominent theologian Albertus Pieters said about this Bible: "One of the most dangerous books in the Christian market".

Cyrus Ingerson Scofield was a lawyer and a politician from Kansas who had to run away from town after being charged with fraud and forgery of legal papers. He left his wife and children and took refuge in Canada. He eventually went back to live in Saint Louis, Missouri, in the U.S. where he became a Christian in one of the services led by D.L. Moody; a year later in 1879 at the age of 36, he was ordained as a minister of the Congregational Church under the leadership of Reverend Goddell, which was a real shock since everyone knew his past well.

Little is known about this man who had such profound influence over the theology and teachings of the Protestant Church. This comes as a surprise, particularly because of the fact that he did not have any kind of theological training on Biblical foundations.

The context of Dispensationalism was given and influenced by these individuals..

The teachings of futurism have a very important place in the Church today and unfortunately all over the world due to the missionaries who were sent overseas from England and the United States.

TEST ALL THINGS AND HOLD ON TO WHAT IS GOOD

In his book *Great prophecies of the Bible,* the co-author Ralph Woodrow writes:

The Roman Catholic Church realized it had to produce a counter interpretation or lose the battle. As the Encyclopedia Britannica says: 'Under the pressure of the Protestant attack new methods emerged from the papal side, with a special mention to the Jesuit Ribera, founder of the futurist school of interpretation'.[5]

***Francisco Ribera** (1537-159) published a 500-page commentary on the essential items about Babylon and the Antichrist with the only intention of discrediting the Protestant teaching that the papacy was the Antichrist. In his book, he wrote that the initial chapters of Revelation referred to the first century. The rest of the chapters were restricted to a literal three-and-a-half-year period at the end times. He taught that the Jewish temple would be rebuilt by an Antichrist, a single individual, who would abolish Christian religion, deny Christ, pretend to be God and conquer the world. When Thomas Brightman (1562-1607), a Protestant learned reformer, saw a copy of Ribera's futurist explanation got angry. "Some time ago they would not let anyone touch a Bible, now they produce a commentary to explain it and take people away from the papal Antichrist".*

The Protestant Church rejected the futurist interpretation for two more centuries. Then, in 1826, Samuel R. Maitland (1792-1866), a librarian to the Archbishop of Canterbury, was the first Protestant who accepted Ribera's futurist view. Ladd writes: "This futurist interpretation with its personal Antichrist and three-and-a-half-year

5   Encyclopedia Britannica, (New York: Encyclopedia Britannica, Inc., 1910), Eleventh edition, Vol. 23, p.213.

tribulation did not take root in the Protestant Church until the beginning of the nineteenth century. S.R. Maitland was the first Protestant who adopted it".[6]

Froom summarizes the situation in these words:

Ribera's commentary laid the foundations of that huge structure called futurism which was built and enlarged by those who followed him until it became the Catholic common position. And later on, marvel of marvels, in the nineteenth century this Jesuit stratagem of interpretation, was finally adopted by an increasing number of Protestants. Futurism, amplified and embellished with the theory of the rapture, has presently become the belief generally accepted by the fundamentalists of popular Protestantism".[7]

Due to all the books about futurist prophecy in circulation today, there is a great deal of speculation on which one of the world leaders will arise as the Antichrist of Bible prophecy. Many Christians are unaware of the old interpretation of the Protestant reformers: that the man of sin rose to power after the fall of the Roman empire and seated above all in the apostate Church and that the papacy was the fulfillment of these things.

Now, brethren, concerning the coming of our Lord Jesus Christ and our gathering together to Him, we ask you, not to be soon shaken in mind or troubled, either by spirit or by word or by letter, as if from us, as though the day of Christ had come. Let no one deceive you by any means; for that Day will not come unless the falling away comes first, and the man of sin is revealed, the son of perdition, who opposes and exalts himself above all

6 George Ladd, The Blessed Hope, (Grand Rapids: Eerdmans, 1956), p.38.
7 Froom, op., cit., Vol.2, p.493.

> *that is called God or that is worshiped, so that he sits as God in the temple of God, showing himself that he is God.*
>
> 2 Thessalonians 2:1-4

> *Therefore, brethren, stand fast and hold the traditions which you were taught, whether by word or our epistle.*
>
> 2 Thessalonians 2:15

Books, videos and films, such as the series *Left behind* by Tim La Haye, the writings of Hal Lindsay, Jack Van Impe and many others, have flooded the market with teachings that exercise influence over the minds of millions of believers through the ideas of futurism and Dispensationalism, Today's Christian television networks abound with teachers that daily propound these teachings so that today they are totally accepted and promoted by huge groups of Christians.

> *As I urged you when I went into Macedonia—remain in Ephesus that you may charge some that they teach no other doctrine, nor give heed to fables and endless genealogies, which cause disputes rather than godly edification which is in faith... from which some, having strayed, have turned aside to idle talk, desiring to be teachers of the law, understanding neither what they say nor the things which they affirm.*
>
> 1 Timothy 1:3-4 and 6-7

A great challenge lies before us: as Christians we must test all things like those in Berea; we must study the Word of God, pay attention to the writings of the patriarchs of the Church and the teachings of the reformers. Many times we analyze the Bible under the influence of our culture and what we hear or read in the mass media of communication.

Despite the historical and biblical evidence presented here, we know a large number of Christians will find it difficult to deal with due to their current beliefs. All progress needs change, and God is changing His Church. The rediscovery of Bible truths has always faced great opposition, even within the Church.

The Protestant Reformation was the starting point of the doctrinal changes in Romanism.

God is bringing back to His Church the Biblical foundations given to the apostles which were contaminated by false teachings by deceivers who abandoned their faith. It is our prayer that the Lord will reveal, by his Holy Spirit, the truths of His Word so that you can become an approved worker who does not need to be ashamed and able to correctly handle and understand the Holy Scriptures.

Gordon Fee a New Testament scholar, author and theologian and Professor Emeritus at Regent College recently commented "You can read the Bible and become a Calvinist, you can read the Bible and become an Armenian, but you can't read the Bible and become a Dispensationalist".

And so we have the prophetic word confirmed, which you do well to heed as a light that shines in a dark place, until the day dawns and the morning star rises in your hearts; knowing this first, that no prophecy of Scripture is of any private interpretation, for prophecy never came by the will of man, but holy men of God spoke as they were moved by the Holy Spirit. 2 Peter 1:19-21

Above all else, however, remember that none of us can explain by ourselves a prophecy in the Scriptures.

2 Peter 1:20, Good News Translation

But you must understand this at the outset, that no prophecy of scripture arose from an individual's interpretation of the truth. 2 Peter 1:20, J. B. Phillips New Testament

Above all, you must realize that no prophecy in Scripture ever came from the prophet's own understanding. 2 Peter 1:20, New Living Translation

2 Peter 1.20 is a warning related to the false teachers in the next chapter; see 2 Peter 3:16.

... as also in all his epistles, speaking in them of these things, in which are some things hard to understand, which untaught and unstable people twist to their own destruction, as they do also the rest of the Scriptures.

2 Peter 3:16

This is what he says in all his letters when he writes on the subject. There are some difficult things in his letters which ignorant and unstable people explain falsely, as they do with other passages of the Scriptures. So they bring on their own destruction. 2 Peter 3:16, Good News Translation

In that letter, as indeed in all his letters, he referred to these matters. There are, of course, some things which are difficult to understand, and which, unhappily, ill-informed and unbalanced people distort (as they do the other scriptures), and bring disaster on their own heads. 2 Peter 3:16, J. B. Phillips New Testament

PART 2

JESUS' PROPHECIES

CHAPTER
3

MATTHEW 24
WHEN WILL
THESE THINGS BE?

*J*esus left the temple and was walking away when his disciples came up to him to call his attention to its buildings. "Do you see all these things?" he asked. "Truly I tell you, not one stone here will be left on another; everyone will be thrown down".–Mathew 24:1-2

TIMES OF PROCESSES AND TIMES OF HAPPENINGS

On that day Jesus made a surprising statement to his disciples. Some of them had shown him the majesty and beauty of the temple in Jerusalem. But the Lord declared that the temple would be completely destroyed and not one stone would be left on another. His words aroused their curiosity to know about the time these things would happen. In order to be able to understand all this in light of the Word, let us have a look at the different versions of these questions in the three gospels with parallel passages:

> *Now as He sat on the Mount of Olives, the disciples came to Him privately, saying: "Tell us, when will these things be? And what will be the sign of your coming, and of the end of the age?" Matthew 24:3*

> *Now as He sat on the Mount of Olives opposite the temple, Peter, James, John, and Andrew asked Him privately: "Tell us, when will these things be? And what will be the sign when all these things will be fulfilled?" Mark 13:3-4*

> *So they asked Him, saying: "Teacher, but when will these things be? And what sign will there be when these things are about to take place?" Luke 21:7*

Today, many Christians interpret the Lord's questions and answers from a futurist point of view before the end of the world.

In the following scriptures the Lord answers the three questions made to him. The interpretation of these replies determines your beliefs about the end times, the tribulation, the Antichrist and the development of future events.

The main question in the three gospels is about the ***destruction of the temple***: When will these things be? When will all this be? (Matthew 24:2)

Matthew 23 describes a day when Jesus was speaking at the temple and rebuked the Pharisees and Scribes; he called them hypocrites and pronounced a severe judgment on them. We read in Matthew 23:36: ***Assuredly, I say to you, all these things will come upon this generation.*** Later on, at the end of his speech in Matthew 24 about the destruction of the temple, Jesus Christ declares: ***Assuredly, I say to you, <u>this generation will by no means pass away till all these things take place</u>" (Matthew 24:34,*** emphasis added by the author).

In Matthew 24:3 we find three different questions:

1. When will these things be?

2. What will be the sign of your coming?

3. And of the end of the age?

By recognizing these three questions and the Lord's three different replies, we will be able to clearly understand the times of each of them. First, Jesus spoke about:

*   ***deceivers***

    And Jesus answered and said to them: "Take heed that no one deceives you. For many will come in My name, saying, 'I am the Christ,' and will deceive many". Matthew 24:4-5

    And He said: "Take heed that you not be deceived. For many will come in My name, saying, 'I

am He,' and, 'the time has drawn near.' Therefore do not go after them". Luke 21:8 (<u>note the time</u>).

And Jesus, answering them, began to say: "Take heed that no one deceives you. For many will come in My name, saying, 'I am He,' and will deceive many". Mark 13:5-6

The three versions mention the word deceivers, but Luke explains "when" these things will occur: *The time has drawn near. Therefore do not go after them.* Jesus Christ was clearly warning them to be careful of something that was about to happen. Undoubtedly, he does not refer to something that would take place hundreds or thousands of years later.

Apostle Paul wrote this warning to the readers in Ephesus:

For I know this, that after my departure savage wolves will come in among you, not sparing the flock. Also from among yourselves men will rise up, speaking perverse things, to draw away the disciples after themselves. Acts 20:29-30

History has proven that this event took place a few years after Jesus' death and resurrection. Josephus, a well known Jewish historian, wrote that twelve years after Christ's death an impostor called Theudas deceived many, by taking them to the Jordan river and declaring that the waters would open before their eyes. An Egyptian pretending to be a Christian prophet gathered about 30,000 men in front of the wall of Jerusalem to show them how it would fall down at his command.

In Acts 8 we read about Simon who deceived many. According to Irenaeus, Simon claimed to be the son of God and the creator of angels; Jerome says that he claimed to be the Word of God, the Almighty and Justin writes that when he came to Rome, he was worshipped as a god for his magical powers.

Felix, who also appears in the book of Acts, declared that the land of the Jews was full of impostors and gave the order to have many of them killed.

There were many other deceivers, among them: Dositheos, Bar-Kokhba and Bar-Jesus (mentioned in Acts 13:6) as Jesus had prophesied.

Then Jesus spoke about:

- *wars and rumors of wars*

  And you will hear of wars and rumors of wars. See that you are not troubled; for all these things must come to pass, but the end is not yet. For nation will rise against nation, and kingdom against kingdom. And there will be famines, pestilences, and earthquakes in various places. Matthew 24: 6-7

  But when you hear of wars and rumors of wars, do not be troubled; for such things must happen, but the end is not yet. For nation will rise against nation, and kingdom against kingdom. And there will be earthquakes in various places, and there will be famines and troubles. These are the beginnings of sorrows. Mark 13:7-8

  But when you hear of wars and commotions, do not be terrified; for these things must come to pass first, but the end will not come immediately. Then

He said to them, Nation will rise against nation,
and kingdom against kingdom. Luke 21:9-10

The Roman empire was enjoying peace within its borders when Jesus Christ shared this prophecy. But soon after that, the whole empire was filled with violence, uprisings and wars within its borders. Before the fall of Jerusalem, in the year 70 A.D. four emperors: Nero, Galba, Otho and Vitellius died in a violent way over a period of eighteen months according to the historian Suetonius.

In the *Annals of Tacitus,* a Roman historian who wrote before the fall of Jerusalem, we find expressions such as "Disturbances in Germania", "commotions in Africa", "insurrections in Gaul", "intrigues among the Parthians", "war in Britannia" and "war in Armenia". In Seleucia more than 50, 000 Jews were killed; more than 20,000 were killed in a war between Jews and Syrians in Caesarea.

Wars and rumors of wars became familiar in nature, but these signs were given to show that the end was NOT yet..

The term "end" does not refer to the
final times but to the end of the Jewish
economy, the destruction of Jerusalem.

This word is *telos* in Greek and means *fulfillment* or *purpose, end of a period.*

Jesus also spoke about:

* *earthquakes, famines and pestilences*

For nation will rise against nation, and king-
dom against kingdom. And there will be famines,

pestilences, and earthquakes in various places. All these are the beginning of sorrows. Matthew 24:7-8

For nation will rise against nation, and kingdom against kingdom. And there will be earthquakes in various places, and there will be famines and troubles. These are the beginnings of sorrows. Mark 13:8

And there will be great earthquakes in various places, and famines and pestilences; and there will be fearful sights and great signs from heaven. Luke 21.11

The Bible speaks about a great famine throughout all the world in the days of Emperor Claudius Caesar; Judea was particularly stricken by famine.

Then one of them, named Agabus, stood up and showed by the Spirit that there was going to be a great famine throughout all the world, which also happened in the days of Claudius Caesar. Then the disciples, each according to his ability, determined to send relief to the brethren dwelling in Judea. Acts 11:28-29

In 1 Corinthians 16: 1-5 and Romans 15: 25-28 we find Paul's instructions about the collection for the "saints".

Historians and patriarchs such as Tacitus, Eusebius and Suetonius speak about great famines in Rome, Judea and Greece a few years before the fall of Jerusalem.

Eusebius writes: *Under the reign of Claudius Caesar the world was visited by a great famine, something about which many authors who are diametrically opposed to our faith wrote in their accounts.*[1]

At the same time, there were great pestilences in Rome in the days of Nero; so severe, that according to history around 30,000 people died under their effect. Josephus also mentions a great pestilence in Babylon in the year 40 A.D.; Tacitus speaks about a pestilence in Italy in the year 66 A.D.

Jesus prophesied:

• *earthquakes*

Tacitus writes that in the years 57 and 58 A.D., there were earthquakes in Rome, in Asia and all around the known world. According to Seneca's writings, the twelve biggest cities in Asia Minor, today known as Turkey, fell because of the destruction of several earthquakes that shook the area.

Great calamities took place due to earthquakes in Syria, Macedonia and Cyprus. In the year 60 A.D., Colossae, Laodicea and Hierapous were greatly destroyed. In the year 63 A.D. the city of Pompeii was destroyed. There were also earthquakes in Crete, Smyrna, Miletus, Samos, Chios, Apamea, Judea and other places.

Jesus spoke about:

• *persecution to the disciples*

Then they will deliver you up to tribulation and kill you, and you will be hated by all nations for

---

1   Church History, II:8

My name's sake. And then many will be offended, will betray one another, and will hate one another. Then many false prophets will rise up and deceive many. Matthew 24:9-11

But when they arrest you and deliver you up, do not worry beforehand, or premeditate what you will speak. But whatever is given you in that hour, speak that; for it is not you who speak, but the Holy Spirit. Now brother will betray brother to death, and a father his child; and children will rise up against parents and cause them to be put to death. And you will be hated by all for My name's sake. But he who endures to the end shall be saved. Mark 13:11-13

But before all these things, they will lay their hands on you and persecute you, delivering you up to the synagogues and prisons. You will be brought before kings and rulers for My name's sake. But it will turn out for you as an occasion for testimony. Therefore settle it in your hearts not to meditate beforehand on what you will answer; for I will give you a mouth and wisdom which all your adversaries will not be able to contradict or resist. You will be betrayed even by parents and brothers, relatives and friends; and they will put some of you to death. And you will be hated by all for My name's sake. Luke 21:12-17

In the book of Acts we find a detailed account of the persecution to the disciples, just like Jesus had predicted: Acts 4:3,7,13,18;

Acts5:18,27,29-32,40,41; Acts 6:9,10,12; Acts7:54-60; Acts 8:1-4; Acts16:22, 23 y 28.

In these verses and others, we can see that the disciples were afflicted, beaten, whipped, imprisoned, persecuted, hated for His name's sake, taken before kings and rulers, delivered into the hands of the Pharisees. "All" these things certainly happened, just like the Lord had prophesied them. It is something that has "already occurred", and not to take place in the future.

Jesus Christ also prophesied:

* *false prophets*

  Then many false prophets will rise up and deceive many. And because lawlessness will abound, the love of many will grow cold. But he who endures to the end shall be saved. Matthew 24:11-13

When Jesus prophesied this, Peter was right there listening to his Master's warning. Later on, Peter points out that this was happening in those days.

> *But there were also false prophets among the people, even as there will be false teachers among you, who will secretly bring in destructive heresies, even denying the Lord who bought them, and bring on themselves swift destruction. And many will follow their destructive ways, because of whom the way of truth will be blasphemed. 2 Peter 2:1-2*

Apostle John wrote his first letter to refute and expose the Gnostics' teachings:

Beloved, do not believe every spirit, but test the spirits, whether they are of God; because many false prophets have gone out into the world. 1 John 4:1

Paul also mentions this situation, probably referring to the Judaizers, and says:

For such are false apostles, deceitful workers, transforming themselves into apostles of Christ. And no wonder! For Satan himself transforms himself into an angel of light. Therefore it is no great thing if his ministers also transform themselves into ministers of righteousness, whose end will be according to their works. 2 Corinthians 11:13-15

I marvel that you are turning away so soon from Him who called you in the grace of Christ, to a different gospel, which is not another; but there are some who trouble you and want to pervert the gospel of Christ. But even if we, or an angel from heaven, preach any other gospel to you than what we have preached to you, let him be accursed. As we have said before, so now I say again, if anyone preaches any other gospel to you than what you have received, let him be accursed. Galatians 1:6-9

And their message will spread like cancer. Hymenaeus and Philetus are of this sort, who have strayed concerning the truth, saying that the resurrection is already past; and they overthrow the faith of some. 2 Timothy 2:17-18

In his letter to his disciple Titus, he called them *idle talkers and deceivers.*

Eusebius writes: ***After the Lord ascended into heaven, the devil released many men who called themselves gods.*** [2]

Likewise, John Wesley declares: ***Therefore, never had the world known so many impostors like a few years before the destruction of Jerusalem, because undoubtedly the Jews were still expecting the Messiah.*** [3]

The true gospel was being contaminated by false teachings, treasons, deceivers and false prophets, and the love of many had grown cold.

But he who endures to the end shall be saved. The word "end" here does not refer to the final days, as it does in Matthew 24:3 where the term is *sunteleia* which means consummation. In verses 6 and 14, we find the word *telos* which means fulfillment of the purpose to the extreme.

Finally Jesus finishes his reply by saying: ***And this gospel of the kingdom will be preached in all the world as a witness to all the nations, and then the end will come. (Matthew 24:14).***

HE WHO STARTED A GOOD WORK WILL BE FAITHFUL TO BRING IT TO AN END

The word "end" (*telos*) here refers to the destruction of Jerusalem and the temple. This is the question posed by the disciples before the Lord. The next verses make the context clear since

---

2   P. Eusebius, Church History, New York, (Harper University Press), 1980, III, p28
3   J Wesley, The Works of John Wesley, 1985

Jesus Christ goes on to speak about the destruction of Jerusalem, the abomination of desolation that Daniel had prophesied many years before, the great tribulation suffered by the Jewish people at the hands of Romans, and the escape from Judea to the mountains of Masada. The fulfillment of the times, the priestly and spiritual order, the law and the decrees.

Many of us who have learnt about futurism take this passage as a challenge to bring the gospel to every nation before the end of times. Let us examine the context of Jesus' words in light of the Bible. If this was truly due to happen during this generation, it should have taken place in the first century.

Were Jesus' words fulfilled? The Lord said: ***Assuredly, I say to you, this generation will by no means pass away till all these things take place (Matthew 24:34).***

No scripture should be of private interpretation; instead we should let the words be interpreted by themselves on the basis of the context of the text.

---

*It can be very easy to take a text out of context
for the sake of our own pretext.*

By doing this, we rule out any risks of mistakes based on our own perceptions or paradigms.

> *... knowing this first, that no prophecy of Scripture is of any private interpretation, for prophecy never came by the will of man, but holy men of God spoke as they were moved by the Holy Spirit.*
> *2 Peter 1:20-21*

We need to study the Word in order to be able to fully understand the passages in Matthew 24:14 and 24:34, which say that all this would take place during that generation and the gospel would be preached in every nation. In the New Testament we find four different passages of how the gospel was preached in every nation of the known world at that time.

First, we see that Paul repeats this several times in the following scriptures:

> *First, I thank my God through Jesus Christ for you all, <u>that your faith is spoken of throughout the whole world.</u> Romans 1:8* (emphasis added by the author)

> *... because of the hope which is laid up for you in heaven, of which you <u>heard before in the word of the truth of the gospel, which has come to you, as it has also in all the world,</u> and is bringing forth fruit, as it is also among you since the day you heard and knew the grace of God in truth. Colossians 1:5-6* (emphasis added by the author)

Paul says that the true Word had come to "all the world". And finally, one of the most clear texts about this subject is in the first letter to the Corinthians:

> *... if indeed you continue in the faith, grounded and steadfast, and are not moved away from the hope of the gospel which you heard, <u>which was preached to every creature under heaven,</u> of which I, Paul, became a minister. Colossians 1.23* (emphasis added by the author)

The text in Greek says: *... and that has been proclaimed to every creature under heaven* (New International Version). *... which was preached in all creation under heaven* (American Standard Version). *... has been preached all over the world* (New Living Translation). *... and which, indeed, the whole world is now having an opportunity of hearing.* (J.B. Phillips, New Testament).

The word *world* in Romans 1:8 and Colossians 1:6 is *kosmos* which can be translated as earth or world. The other Greek word for world is *oikoumene* which means inhabited world or civilized land. That is the reason why we read in Acts 17:6: *These who have turned the world upside down have come here too.*

This is the interpretation of some of the apostolic fathers:

Justin Martyr: ***From Jerusalem, men who were twelve in number and many others went out to the whole world; they were illiterate, uneducated, with no ability to speak in public but by the power of God they proclaimed the gospel to the entire human race to which they were sent by Christ to teach about the true God in all the world.***[4]

Eusebius: ***Soon after the teaching of the new covenant was taken to all nations, the Romans laid siege to Jerusalem and destroyed it, together with the temple.***[5]

C H Spurgeon: ***It was just before that generation passed away that Jerusalem was besieged and destroyed. There was an interval which was long enough for the total preaching of the gospel by the apostles and evangelists of the early Church, and for the going out of all those who recognized Christ as the true Messiah. Then the horrendous end came, which had been***

---

4   J. Martyr, First Apology, XXXIX, in the Ante-Nicene Fathers, Translation of the Fathers until 325 A.D.

5   Eusebius, Proof of the Gospel. I:VI

prophesied by the Savior and the terrible mourning which came over that guilty capital.[6]

Flavius Josephus: *A generation takes 40 years. Jesus Christ prophesied this about the year 33 A.D., which means all this would happen before the year 73 A.D. According to history, in the year 70 A.D., the Roman general Titus destroyed Jerusalem with more than 20,000 Roman soldiers. Titus laid siege to the city and cut the food supplies so that the people would starve to death. After four months they invaded the city and killed more than a million Jews. The soldiers set the temple on fire and destroyed it, capturing and enslaving 97,000 people.*[7]

Many books describe the fall of Jerusalem in detail, but perhaps the most important one is the work of the Jewish historian Flavius Josephus, called *Wars of the Jews.* Among the fathers of the Church who have written about this subject we can mention:

Origen from Alexandria: *I challenge anyone to prove me wrong when I say that the whole Jewish nation was destroyed in less than a generation due to the suffering they inflicted on Jesus. For this reason I believe there were 42 years between Jesus' crucifixion and the destruction of Jerusalem.*[8]

Eusebius: *And all this took place in this way in the second year of Vespasian' reign (70 A.D.) according to the predictions of the Savior, Jesus Christ.*[9]

John Wesley: *This was punctually fulfilled: after the burning of the temple, by order of Titus, the Roman general, the foundations of the temple were excavated and later devastated*

---

6   C H Spurgeon, The Gospel of the Kingdom. P.218
7   Flavius Josephus, Wars of the Jews, vi:ix3
8   Against Celsus, IV:XXII
9   P. Eusebius, Church History, 1980 (Harper University Press) III:p7

by Turnus Rufus. The expression <u>that generation of men will not pass away until these things have taken place</u>... was true. The city and the temple were destroyed 39 or 40 years later.[10]

In the next chapter we will continue to explain the second question that the disciples asked Jesus in Matthew 24:

What will be the sign of your coming?

---

10   The Works of John Wesley, 1985

CHAPTER
4

MATTHEW 24 AND WHAT WILL BE THE SIGN OF YOUR COMING?

THE THINGS TO COME

The disciples' second question to Jesus was about his coming as King of Israel. Up to the moment of the question, there had not been indication of the second coming of the Lord in the Jewish Torah. They asked about the sign of his coming as Messiah, King of Israel, to sit on the throne and reign over his people. Reading this question, we could easily misinterpret the disciple's thoughts at that time. At that point in Christ's ministry, they did not have the certainty that their Lord was going to die, let alone be raised and ascend into heaven to sit at the right hand of the Father for thousands of years and come back later.

In their excellent book *Victorious Eschatology*, Harold Eberle and Martin Trench explain that the disciples' question had to do mainly with his triumphal entry as King of Israel into the city of Jerusalem. "When will you take your place and be revealed as King?" "When will you come to reign?"

Perhaps we need to have a look at Apostle Luke's gospel in order to be able to clearly understand the nature of the second question, which is about the *sign* of the beginning of the general things that he had just described for them: *And what sign will there be when these things are about to take place? (Luke 21:7b).*

Before that, Jesus had declared that some of them would not die without seeing him as King first:

> **And He said to them: "Assuredly, I say to you that there are some standing here who will not taste death till they see the kingdom of God present with power". Mark 9:1**

> **For the Son of Man will come in the glory of His Father with His angels, and then He will reward each according to his works. Assuredly, I say to you, there are some standing here who shall not taste death till they see the Son of Man coming in His kingdom. Matthew 16:27-28**

The mother of Zebedee's sons had asked Jesus if when he entered his Kingdom as King, her sons might sit one on his right and the other on the left (Matthew 20:20-23).

The Lord's reply was very clear. Some of them who were there would still be alive when he came into his Kingdom, not more than 2,000 years later. Jesus Christ's answer without a doubt did NOT refer to a distant future.

In his book *The History of Redemption* Jonathan Edwards writes: *It is clear that when Jesus speaks about his return, being revealed, the coming into his Kingdom, the coming of his Kingdom, He does it in relation to the appearance of great works of power, justice and grace. It would happen in the destruction of Jerusalem and other extraordinary providences.*[1]

This was Jesus Christ's answer to the question:

> ***Therefore when you see the <u>abomination of desolation</u>, spoken of by Daniel the prophet, standing in the holy place (whoever reads, let him understand), then let those who are in Judea flee to the mountains. Let him who is on the housetop not go down to take anything out of his house. And let him who is in the field not go back to get his clothes. But woe to those who are pregnant and to those who are nursing babies in those days! And pray that your flight may not be in winter or on the Sabbath. For then there will be <u>great tribulation</u>, such as has not been since the beginning of the world until this time, no, nor ever shall be. And unless those days were shortened, no flesh would be saved; but for the elect's sake those days will be shortened. Matthew 24:15-22 (emphasis added by the author)***

These two events would be the sign of his coming as King into his kingdom. The abomination of desolation, mentioned by Daniel, was undoubtedly referring to the destruction of the temple, of which not one stone would be left on another, and the total destruction of Jerusalem.

---

1   J. Edwards, The History of Redemption, 1776, Miscellanea #1199

Let us read what Daniel says:

> *Seventy weeks are determined for your people and for your holy city, to finish the transgression, to make an end of^{sins}, to make reconciliation for iniquity, to bring in everlasting righteousness, to seal up vision and prophecy, and to anoint the Most Holy. Know therefore and understand, that from the going forth of the command to restore and build Jerusalem until Messiah the Prince, there shall be seven weeks and sixty-two weeks; the street shall be built again, and the wall, even in troublesome times. And after the sixty-two weeks Messiah shall be cut off, but not for Himself; and the people of the prince who is to come shall destroy the city and the sanctuary. The end of it shall be with a flood, and till the end of the war desolations are determined. Then he shall confirm a covenant with many for one week; but in the middle of the week He shall bring an end to sacrifice and offering. and on the wing of abominations shall be one who makes desolate, even until the consummation, which is determined, is poured out on the desolate. Daniel 9:24-27*

Verse 24 speaks about 70 weeks, or 490 years, over the Jewish order and Jerusalem at the end of which sin would be finished and the expiatory payment for iniquity would take place through the Messiah's death. Christ's blood shedding and his death would result in a remission because it would cancel the need for animal sacrifices: expiation of transgressions and everlasting justice. (Hebrews 9:15, 16, 22, 28; 10:10-18).

This is the description of this 490-year period in a commentary of the Spirit Filled bible:

9.24, 26 The seventy weeks, or "seventy times seven years" is a prophetic term related to Daniel's people, the Jews, and the holy city of Jerusalem. The fact that the week of years (490 years) is made of years of 360 days is proven by comparing 7.25 with Revelation 11:2, 3; 12:6, 14 y 13:5.

The counting of weeks of years starts with Artajerjes' command in 445 B.C. to restore Jerusalem. The period is chronologically divided into:

Seven times seven — 49 years: from 445 to 396 B.C.

(From Artajerjes' decree to Nehemiah's arrival and the celebration of the covenant renewal in Jerusalem).

Sixty-two times seven — 434 years: from 396 B.C. to 32 A.D.

(From the dedication of the second temple to our Lord Jesus Christ's crucifixion).[2]

Daniel 9:26 refers to how a prince, the Roman Caesar, would put Jesus of Nazareth to death, and not only would he have Christ crucified but he would also destroy the temple and the city of Jerusalem before a generation later (70 A.D.).

When Jesus mentioned the abomination of desolation, he was referring to the destruction of the temple and of Jerusalem.

---

2   Hayford, Jack W., General Editor, Spirit Filled Bible, (Nashville, TN: Editorial Caribe) 2000, c1994.

24.15 The author of the apocryphal book 1 Maccabeus (1:54, 59; 6:7) related the abomination of desolation, prophesied in Daniel (9:27; 11:31; 12:11), to the desecration of the temple in the year 168 B.C. by the Syrian ruler Antiochus Epiphanes. However, for Jesus the prophecy referred to another desecration: the arrival of the Roman army which besieged Jerusalem and destroyed the temple in the year 70 A.D. This event foretells the conditions associated with Christ's return, so that the prophecy awaits its last consummation in a way which is not described in the Scriptures.[3]

Apostles Mark and Luke wrote the following words:

> ***But when you see Jerusalem surrounded by armies, and then know that its desolation is near. Then let those who are in Judea flee to the mountains, let those who are in the midst of her depart, and let not those who are in the country enter her. For these are the days of vengeance, that all things which are written may be fulfilled. But woe to those who are pregnant and to those who are nursing babies in those days! For there will be great distress in the land and wrath upon this people. And they will fall by the edge of the sword, and be led away captive into all nations. And Jerusalem will be trampled by Gentiles until the times of the Gentiles are fulfilled. Luke 21:20-24***
>
> ***So when you see the 'abomination of desolation', spoken of by Daniel the prophet, standing where it ought not (let the reader understand), then let those who are in Judea flee to the mountains. Let him***

---

3   Hayford, Jack W., General Editor, Spirit Filled Bible, (Nashville, TN: Editorial Caribe) 2000, c1994.

who is on the housetop not go down into the house,
nor enter to take anything out of his house. And
let him who is in the field not go back to get his
clothes. But woe to those who are pregnant and to
those who are nursing babies in those days! Mark
13:14-17 (emphasis added by the author)

Matthew and Mark say that they would see the abomination of desolation mentioned by the prophet Daniel. In the context of the Bible we never see that this event would take place over 2,000 years later. I repeat, when Jesus said: *when you see,* he was specifically addressing them. This was Daniel's prophecy: *and the people of the prince who is to come shall destroy the city and the sanctuary.*

By comparing these parallel passages, we can understand the nature of the second question; and Christ's reply was that the *sign* would be the destruction of Jerusalem at the hands of the Roman armies in the year 70 A.D, just as history tells us.

Before this occurred all the Christians who lived there, in obedience to Jesus' command, fled from Jerusalem to escape from the horrible judgment that fell upon the city and its inhabitants. The account of this event is truly amazing.

In the year 65 A.D., Florus, the worst Roman procurator, assumed control of Judea. His violent and cruel actions provoked a rebellion and insurgency among the Jews. Cestius Gallus was sent to take over and marched with his armies into Palestine destroying and subduing several communities before their entry into Jerusalem.[4]

When they saw that Jerusalem was surrounded by the Roman armies and the destruction of the city was imminent, the abomination of desolation Jesus Christ had warned them about, they understood it was the moment to flee from there. But, how

---

4   Josephus, Jewish War II. Chapters 15-19

could they possibly be able to do this if the city was completely surrounded? This is what happened:

All of a sudden and without any reason, Cestius withdrew his army and they departed. This encouraged the Jews to pursue the retreating army causing great damage to it.[5]

Thomas Newton describes clearly what happened with the Christians living in Jerusalem during this brief period of time:

We learn from the Church accounts that at this time all the believers in Christ left from Jerusalem to several regions beyond the Jordan; for that reason they were all marvelously able to escape from the tragedy of their fellow countrymen and we do not read anywhere that a single one of them perished in the destruction of Jerusalem.[6]

Adam Clark says: *It is amazing that not even a single Christian perished in the destruction of Jerusalem although many of them were living there during the time Celsius Gallus devastated the city. A truly remarkable escape. What a confirmation of our Savior's words! A surprising fulfillment of his prophecy.[7]*

MYTHS AND WRONG BELIEFS ABOUT THE GREAT TRIBULATION

The futurist theory teaches that the abomination of desolation is an idol, possibly of the Antichrist or the Antichrist himself, which will be put in the most holy place of a rebuilt Jewish temple.

---

5   Ibid. 19.5-8
6   Newton, Dissertations on the Prophecies. P.389. Eusebius, Church History. Book 3, Chap. 5. Edersheim, Life and Time of Jesus the Messiah. P.448
7   Clarke's Commentaries. Vol. 1, Matthew-Acts, p228

This theories teach that it will take place in the "future", which is a meaningless interpretation.

More people perished in the destruction of Jerusalem than due to the two atomic bombings in Japan, during the second World War. The city fell, the nation no longer existed and the temple was totally destroyed; this was the "sign" of the end of the Jewish people as a nation and as a government system. This is what Jesus referred to when he mentioned "the end".

With the destruction of the temple, the religious system of the nation came to an end. There was no longer expiation through animal sacrifices in the temple and priests were not able to go into the Holy of Holies in favor of the people's sins. A new Holy Priest came to reign. The stone rejected by the builders was then the foundation of a new temple made of living stones. Jesus had started to rule from his heavenly throne over his everlasting Kingdom. David's throne was replaced by the heavenly throne.[8]

Jesus' reply to the second question finishes with a crucial declaration: ***Assuredly, I say to you, this generation will by no means pass away till all these things take place. Heaven and earth will pass away, but My words will by no means pass away (Matthew 24:34-35).***

Given the importance of the subject of *The great tribulation*, although it belongs to the second question, I will explain later on in detail the interpretation of Jesus' reply about this matter.

Everybody agrees to the fact that a biblical generation represents a 40-year period. This means that we should take Jesus' words literally, let the Bible explain by itself and avoid any attempt to interpret it in a different way in order to provide an

---

8   H. Eberle y M. Trench. Victorious Eschatology, p.66

alternative context. If we accept Jesus' prophecy in Matthew 24:5-35, then we must admit that all this happened before the destruction of the temple and the holy city of Jerusalem in the year 70 A.D.

Futurism is obviously forced to define the word generation (Gr. *genesis)* as race which does not match the commonly recognized and accepted definition. This word appears 34 times in the New Testament and is *never* interpreted as *race.*

This is what John Calvin comments about this:

Christ announces that before a generation came to pass, they would have learnt from experience what he had told them. Less than fifty years later the city was destroyed, the temple was eradicated and the whole land was reduced to a horrible desert.[9]

---

9   J. Calvin's Commentaries, A Harmony of the Gospels Matthew, Luke and Mark. Vol. 3, p.151

Chapter 5

THE GREAT TRIBULATION

WHAT SIGN WILL THERE BE OF YOUR COMING?

For then there will be great tribulation, such as has not been since the beginning of the world until this time, no, nor ever shall be. And unless those days were shortened, no flesh would be saved; but for the elect's sake those days will be shortened.

–Matthew 24:21-22

For in those days there will be tribulation, such as has not been since the beginning of the creation which God created until this time, nor ever shall be. And unless the Lord had shortened those days, no flesh would be saved; but for the elect's sake, whom He chose, He shortened the days.–Mark 13:19-20

For these are the days of vengeance, that all things which are written may be fulfilled. But woe to those who are pregnant and to those who are nursing babies in those days! For there will be great distress in the land and wrath upon this people. And they will fall by the edge of the sword, and be led away captive into all nations. And Jerusalem will be trampled by Gentiles until the times of the Gentiles are fulfilled.–Luke 21:22-24

IN THE LAST DAYS...

We are forced to ignore the context of Jesus' words in order to reach the futurist conclusion of a period known as the *great tribulation* which Luke calls great distress or affliction.

These parallel verses interpret the word *thlipsis* (#2437 in the Strong's Concordance) in different ways. The term appears 38 times in the New Testament and is translated as *tribulation, affliction, distress, retribution, vengeance, anguish, worry and calamity.*

In the book of Luke we find a clear explanation of these times of retribution, affliction or tribulation. Great suffering in the land (Judea) and wrath over this people (Jewish); they will be killed by the sword (the siege of Jerusalem and Masada) and will be taken captives (more than 90,000) to every nation; Jerusalem will be downtrodden by the Gentiles until their times are fulfilled (in reference to the destruction of Jerusalem at the hands of the Gentiles).

Josephus, the great Jewish historian who was an eye witness and was present at all these events before and after the destruction of Jerusalem, wrote a detailed account called *Wars of the Jews*, only five years after these things happened. Josephus was not a converted believer, so he could not have manipulated his descriptions and details to prove Jesus' prophecies. It is interesting that he uses such words as: *great tribulation, unspeakable calamities, ruthless destruction, terrible atrocities and horrible bloodshed.* Josephus uses all these expressions, and many others, to describe the desolation and destruction that the Romans brought over the Jewish people during the siege of Judea, Jerusalem and Masada. Chapters two, three, four and six have all the details.

This is the description in the historian's own words:

The calamities that fell upon the Jews were "the greatest" of all, not only in our age but the kind never seen in a war of a city against a city or a nation against a nation... It seems that man's misfortunes from the beginning of time cannot be compared to the ones that came upon the Jews.[1]

The Christian translator of Josephus' work added the following words in a reference: *These calamities that befell upon the Jews, who sacrificed our Savior, were the greatest ever; this is what our Savior had predicted and was fulfilled to such an extent that Josephus proves to be the most authentic witness.[2]*

The book of Isaiah, also known as "the fifth gospel", begins with a prophecy that seems to depict in detail the happenings

---

1   F. Josephus, Wars of the Jews, Preface. P.427
2   Ibíd. P. 429

of the Jewish people, the nation of Israel, the land of Judea and
Jesus' words about future events:

> *Hear, O heavens, and give ear, O earth! For
> the Lord has spoken: "I have nourished and
> brought up children, and they have rebelled
> against Me; the ox knows its owner and the don-
> key its master's crib; but Israel does not know,
> my people do not consider." Alas, sinful nation,
> a people laden with iniquity, a brood of evildoers,
> children who are corrupters! They have forsaken
> the Lord, they have provoked to anger the Holy
> One of Israel, they have turned away backward.
> Your country is desolate, your cities are burned
> with fire; strangers devour your land in your pres-
> ence; and it is desolate, as overthrown by strang-
> ers. So the daughter of Zion is left as a booth in a
> vineyard, as a hut in a garden of cucumbers, as a
> besieged city. Unless the Lord of hosts had left to
> us a very small remnant, we would have become
> like Sodom, we would have been made like Go-
> morrah. Isaiah 1:2-4, 7-9*

THE GOD OF WRATH VS. THE GOD OF LOVE

The explanation given by futurism about the period of *catching up* or *rapture* is that we have not been appointed to wrath
(1 Thessalonians 5:9), that Jesus will deliver us from wrath (1
Thessalonians 1:10), that God's wrath comes over the children of
disobedience (Colossians 3:6), that we will be saved from wrath
(Romans 5:9), that God's wrath is poured out to destroy the
world (Revelation 14:10, 15:1), and other similar verses. But, is

this a correct interpretation of the word "tribulation"? Do Jesus and the authors of the New Testament promise a life where there will not be affliction or tribulation?

According to dispensationalism, the great tribulation that is to come upon the earth will be caused by the Antichrist.

They interpret the word *wrath* as destruction, damage, persecution, etc., at the hands of this character. However, the expression *the wrath* usually refers to the judgment or the payment of God, not the Antichrist; and although it is true that God is with us and never leaves or forsakes us, it is also a fact that in this world in which we live we will go through tribulation because of our faith.

I believe that the Bible, far from avoiding suffering, clearly describes the opposite. We need to do a detailed study of the word *thlipsis,* which is interpreted in different ways, in order to be able to understand and come to a right conclusion about Jesus' words.

In the scriptures we have already seen: Matthew 24:21 and 29, Mark 13:19 and 24, Luke 21:23-24, the word is used four times in reference to the Jewish people. All these things had their fulfillment in the year 70 A.D.

The word also appears 32 times in reference to the believers. Unlike the futurist teachings of Dispensationalism, we can see that Jesus' words do promise tribulation for Christians as something "inevitable".

These things I have spoken to you, that in Me you may have peace. In the world you will have tribulation; but be of good cheer, I have overcome the world. John 16:33

We must through many tribulations (thlipsis) enter the kingdom of God. Acts 14:22

And not only that, but we also glory in tribulations (thlipsis), knowing that tribulation (thlipsis) produces perseverance. Romans 5:3

Who shall separate us from the love of Christ? Shall tribulation, or distress, or persecution, or famine, or nakedness, or peril, or sword? Romans 8:35

In 2 Corinthians 7:4, Paul writes that he rejoices in tribulations (thlipsis); the apostle encourages us to be patient in tribulation (Romans 12:12), to endure tribulation (2 Thessalonians 1:4), not to lose heart in tribulation (Ephesians 3:13); and he says that the Lord comforts us in our tribulations so that we may be able to comfort those who are in tribulation (2 Corinthians 1:4). Matthew 13:21 mentions the phrase "when tribulation arises (thlipsis)".

John says that he is the companion of all believers in tribulation (Revelation 1:9); in Revelation 7:14, referring to "all" believers of all nations, languages and peoples, he writes that they "come out of the great tribulation". This is the Spirit Filled Bible commentary about this:

Revelation 7.14 *"the ones who come out": expresses a repeated and continuous action, not a single one. This is not a picture of the consummation of history; therefore, tribulation is something that occurs, to a certain extent, during the whole existence of the Church (see 1:9, 2:9-22; Matthew 13:21; John 16:33; Acts 14:22; Romans 8:35-36, 12:12).*

This word is also translated as affliction, adversity, anguish, calamity, sorrow, misery, suffering, breaking, hard times. In all these cases it makes reference to the tribulations, afflictions and adversities that Christian believers go through.

Additionally, the word *thlipsis* is translated twice as tribulation in reference to the punishment of the evil doers.

> *... tribulation and anguish, on every soul of man who does evil, of the Jew first and also of the Greek. Romans 2:9*
>
> *... since it is a righteous thing with God to repay with tribulation those who trouble you. 2 Thessalonians 1:6*

Are we saying that there will not be tribulation at the end times?

Throughout the centuries, there have always been times of tribulation for Christians in different ways and for various reasons.

We cannot guarantee that the last days will be the exception. But we do not believe that the great tribulation, as defined by futurists, will take place just as they describe it.

Jesus Christ compared the end times to what happened in the days of Noah and Lot: they were eating, selling, buying, planting, building, getting married, working, sleeping, cooking, etc.

Everything is a normal routine and, all of a sudden, one will be taken and another will be left. Regardless of how it happens, we are called to be always ready.

In the chapter about the rapture or catching up, we have a clear explanation of this event. If we understand this from the point of view of the context, unbelievers will be taken by death, by "sudden destruction" which will come with the Lord when he returns (1 Thessalonians 5:3). On the contrary, those who believe in Christ will be left, their lives will be saved. That is a completely different order to the one suggested by dispensationalism in their explanation about the so-called "rapture of the Church". If we are going to be caught up before the glorious appearance of our Savior Jesus Christ, then Paul inspired by the Holy Spirit made a serious mistake when he wrote:

> *For the grace of God that brings salvation has appeared to all men, teaching us that, denying ungodliness and worldly lusts, we should live soberly, righteously, and godly in the present age, looking for the blessed hope and glorious appearing of our great God and Savior Jesus Christ. Titus 2:11-13*

PART 3

THE PROPHECIES

Chapter 6

DANIEL'S PROPHECY – THE LITTLE HORN

THE BEAST, THE MARK OF THE BEAST, 666

fter this I saw in the night visions, and behold, a fourth beast, dreadful and terrible, exceedingly strong. It had huge iron teeth; it was devouring, breaking in pieces, and trampling the residue with its feet. It was different from all the beasts that were before it, and it had ten horns. I was considering the horns, and there was another horn, a little one, coming up among them, before whom three of the first horns were plucked out by the roots. And there, in this horn, were eyes like the eyes of a man, and a mouth speaking pompous words.–Daniel 7:7-8

I was watching; and the same horn was making war against the saints, and prevailing against them, until the Ancient of Days came, and a judgment was made in favor of the saints of the Most High, and the time came for the saints to possess the kingdom. Thus he said: 'The fourth beast shall be a fourth kingdom on earth, which shall be different from all other kingdoms, and shall devour the whole earth, trample it and break it in pieces. The ten horns are ten kings who shall arise from this kingdom. And another shall rise after them; he shall be different from the first ones, and shall subdue three kings. He shall speak pompous words against the Most High, shall persecute the saints of the Most High, and shall intend to change times and law. Then the saints shall be given into his hand for a time and times and half a time. But the court shall be seated, and they shall take away his dominion, to consume and destroy it forever. Then the kingdom and dominion, and the greatness of the kingdoms under the whole heaven, shall be given to the people, the saints of the Most High. His kingdom is an everlasting kingdom, and all dominions shall serve and obey Him'.–Daniel 7:21-27

FOUR POWERFUL KINGDOMS

In a vision Daniel saw four big beasts symbolizing four kingdoms that would rise on earth (Daniel 7):

1. *The first was like a lion, and had eagle's wings. I watched till its wings were plucked off* (Daniel 7:4). The first empire in Dan-

iel's vision, just like the lion is the king of the jungle among animals, was Babylon. The fact that its wings were plucked off means that this powerful kingdom fell in the end.

2. *And suddenly another beast, a second, like a bear. It was raised up on one side, and had three ribs in its mouth* (Daniel 7:5). The second, the Medo-Persian kingdom had less glory, just like the bear is less ferocious and noble than the lion. This did not enjoy so much riches or luxury; neither did they have so much splendor. The mentioning of three ribs in the mouth –between the teeth, where a bear crushes its prey– can refer to the fact that they trampled on the three provinces the kingdom of Babylon was made up of: Babylon, Libya and Egypt.

3. *After this I looked, and there was another, like a leopard, which had on its back four wings of a bird* (Daniel 7:6). The symbol of the third kingdom, Alexander the Great's *Greek empire,* is the leopard with its characteristic agile movements and its extraordinary fast speed to hunt its prey. Likewise, Alexander's conquests were incredibly fast. According to history at the age of 32 he had already conquered the entire world and was sorry that there were no more places to be reached.

The four heads of the leopard probably represent the four kingdoms that ascended to the throne after Alexander's death:

(1) Cassander in Greece and the nearby territory;

(2) Lysimachus in Asia Minor;

(3) Seleucus in Syria and Babylon; and

(4) Ptolemy in Egypt.

4. The fourth beast Daniel saw was *dreadful and terrible, exceedingly strong. It had huge iron teeth; it was devouring, breaking in pieces, and trampling the residue with its feet. It was different from all the beasts that were before it, and it had ten horns* (Daniel 7:7). The fourth world kingdom, different from all the other kingdoms in history, was *the Roman Empire.* Just as it was prophesied, it was dreadful, terrible and strong because it trampled on the entire world. Verse 24 explains the meaning of the ten horns of this beast: *The ten horns are ten kings* (or kingdoms) *that shall arise from this kingdom.* Machiavelli, the Roman historian, wrote that this empire was divided into ten Gothic tribes: Heruli, Serbs, Burgundies, Huns, Ostrogoths, Visigoths, Vandals, Lombards, Franks and Anglo-Saxons. Since then they have been known as the ten kingdoms which arose from the Roman Empire.

THE REVELATION OF THE "LITTLE HORN"

Daniel continues to say: ***I was considering the horns, and there was another horn, a little one, coming up among them, before whom three of the first horns were plucked out by the roots. And there, in this horn, were eyes like the eyes of a man, and a mouth speaking pompous words (v 8); and the same horn was making war against the saints (v 21); and shall intend to change times and law. (V 25).*** This little horn shows eight characteristics in total:

1. It would be a *Roman* power. The horn of a beast comes out of the animal. If the fourth beast was Roman, so must be the horn. Is this a description of the Roman Emperors and after the fall of the Roman Empire the papal office that replaced it? It is!

No one can argue the fact that the papacy is Roman. Its seat is situated in Rome. Its name is *Roman* Catholic Church, quite an amazing point of reference even these days.

2. The little horn would exercise its great power among the ten kingdoms into which the Roman Empire was divided. The papacy rose to power among these ten kingdoms, after the fall of Rome.

3. Three of the other horns would be defeated by the little horn (Daniel 7:24). Did the papacy defeat three of these ten kingdoms? Elliott writes: *I can mention three from the first list, which were eradicated before the Pope: the Heruli under Odaacer, the Vandals and the Ostrogoths.*[33] The Heruli fell in 493, the Vandals in 534 and the Ostrogoths in 553.

4. Although the little horn was going to come up among the ten horns (kingdoms), it would be different. Has the papacy been a different kingdom from the ones risen from the fourth beast? It has. While other kingdoms had control only of the political power, the papacy seized control also of the spiritual power.

The papacy is the only government risen from the ruins of the Roman Empire; for that reason it stood out like the sun in comparison with the moon.

---

1   [33] Elliott, op.cit., Vol. 3, p.139.

This is Guinness' explanation:

Is the papacy not different enough from all the other king-doms in Western Europe as to identify it as the little horn? What other ruling monarch of Christendom ever pretended to have apostolic authority, or ruled over men in the name of God? Does the Pope dressed in royal robes? No, but in priestly garments. Does he wear a crown? No, but a triple tiara to show that he reigns in heaven, earth and hell! Does he wield a scepter? No, but a crosier or crook to show that he is the good shepherd of the Church. Do his subjects kiss his hand? No, but his toe. In fact, this power is different, both in big and small details. It is small in size but gigantic in his pretentions!

5. Daniel saw that the little horn had a mouth that spoke *great words against the Most High* (Daniel 7:20,25). This is an indication of his pride and arrogance. The papacy has spoken against God through its corrupt doctrines. The prophecy declares what this little horn *is going to do*, not what it *professes to do*. It professes to proclaim God's words and define his doctrines; but in reality, he speaks things that are unscriptural and, in some cases, are in to-tal opposition to the Word of God.

    The popes have made many big statements, such as the *Unam Sanctam* bull issued by Boniface VIII with special arrogance: "In order to attain salvation, all the faithful of Christ must be subject to the Roman pontiff who judges all mankind… Therefore we declare, assert, define and pronounce that it is absolutely *necessary for the salvation* of every human being to be subject to the Roman pontiff".

2   [34] Guinness, op.cit., p.28.

With his mouth, the Pope has made statements that no bishop had ever made before. His declarations are final, his utterances infallible; his decrees irreformable.

6. The little horn in Daniel's vision *had eyes and a mouth which spoke pompous words, whose appearance was greater than his fellows* (Daniel 7:20). The horn of a beast has no eyes; that is why its symbolism is so striking. This horn would be a power with prevision and intelligence. It would be able "to see everything" with its eyes. Does it apply to the power of the papacy? The Pope declares that he supervises the Church all around the world and that he is the caretaker and shepherd of more people than any other leader. He is superior to his fellow ministers, who fear him because he claims to have the keys of the kingdom of heaven. His declarations are considered to be the final word; his words are infallible and his decrees, irrefutable.

7. The little horn would *make war and wear out the saints of the Most High* (Daniel 7:21,25). The Jews persecuted the early Christians; later on they were persecuted by the kingdom of the pagan Roman Empire. But the war against the saints here described would be carried out by a power that would arise from Rome. History shows that century after century, Christians suffered persecution at the hands of a power that rose out of Rome. First under the hands of the Roman Emperor and subsequently at the hands of the power of the Papacy.

Now the beast which I saw was like a leopard, his feet were like the feet of a bear. And his mouth like the mouth of a

*lion. The dragon gave him his power, his throne and great
authority. And I saw one of his heads as if it had been mor-
tally wounded and his deadly wound was healed. And all the
world marveled and followed the beast. So they worshipped
the dragon who gave authority to the beast, saying, "Who is
like the beast? Who is able to make war with him? And he
was given a mouth speaking great things and blasphemies,
and he was given authority to continue for 42 months. Then
he opened his mouth in blasphemy against God, to blaspheme
His name, His tabernacle and those that dwell in heaven. It
was granted him to make war with the saints and to overcome
them. And authority was given him over every tribe, tongue,
and nation. All who dwell on the earth will worship him
whose names have not been written in the Book of Life of the
Lamb slain from the foundation of the world. Rev. 13.2-8*

John writes that he would make war against the saints
for a period of 42 months. *"Nero's persecution against the
Church started in 64 A. D. and was the first roman attack
against Christianity, as noted by many of the Church patriarchs amongst them, Eusebius, Tertullian, Sulspicius Severus
as well as roman historians Tacitus and Suetonius"*[3] Nero
was assassinated with a sword on June 8 of 68 A.D., and
that ended the bloody persecution against the believers.
Exactly 42 months of persecution as prophesied by the
Apostle John in Rev.13.5.

During the following centuries Rome and the Roman
Church horribly tortured, tested and judged every Christian who did not bow down to the Roman rulers or accept
the Greatest Pontiff's statements. Pope Innocent IV issued
a bull where he said that those heretics had to be crushed

---

3   K.L. Gentry, Jr. He Shall Have Dominion. TX, Dominion, pp377-78

like venomous snakes. Soldiers were promised property and the remission of all their sins if they killed a heretic!. The "rack" was a torture device where the victims of the Inquisition were stretched and torn apart. Some were crushed and stabbed to death on the "iron virgins". The "thumbscrew" was a device to have the fingers disarticulated and crushed; the "Spanish boots" were used to crush the legs and feet. They also had their nails pulled out with pinchers, or red-hot placed in sensitive parts of the body.

Many torture devices imagined by evil men were used. Those who would not be subject to the papal system were shut up in caves and dungeons, nailed to trees, tormented with fire, scalded with boiling oil or tar. Melted lead was poured into their eyes, ears and mouths; they were scalped and skinned alive; their heads were twisted off and their eyes gouged out. Women suffered mutilation by having their breasts cut off ; babies were brutally beaten, stabbed and thrown against trees or at hungry dogs and swine in front of their parents. It is estimated that during those centuries, papal persecution had more than fifty million Christians were killed. This period is also known as "the Inquisition".

If "prevailing or wearing out the saints of the Most High" does not refer to these methods of torture applied from generation to generation, what else could it be?

In comparison with the Inquisition, all the other persecutions were brief and mild.

However, according to the futurist interpretation the Antichrist will be a super politician who will drop highly destructive bombs from jet planes. This is what one writer says: *Antichrist will plunge the nations into the last great atomic war.*[4]The Bible does not refer to that in this passage. If bombs were dropped over cities, they would kill saints and sinners; in fact, this kind of war would obviously take the lives of more sinners than Christians. But the war in Daniel chapter 7 would not be a massive destruction of human beings, but a war specifically declared against the *saints*!

• 8. The little horn *shall intend to change times and law* (Daniel 7:25). Daniel said that God is the one that *changes the times and the seasons* (Daniel 2:21). But "this little horn" even dares to even meddle in *divine* things!. Changing only civil laws would not be so serious; politicians do it all the time. But tampering with divine laws and precepts demonstrates his blasphemous character.

As to human laws, the papacy has annulled kings and emperors' decrees. It has brought rulers to its knees in abject humility. As to religious matters, the Pope declares that his teachings in doctrine are infallible and millions of people have believed this dogma of his exalted position, which reveals the fact that the papacy appeared with the intention of changing God's laws. For example, they have set the observance of certain days where there is no scriptural basis and instituted rituals and rites derived from paganism; and then declared themselves as the final authority in matters of Christian doctrine.

---

4   [35] M.R. De Haan, Will the Church Go Through the Tribulation? (Grand Rapids: Radio Bible Class), p.25.

According to the Bible, the little horn would be a Roman power that would rise among the ten kingdoms into which the empire was divided, overthrow three of the other kingdoms, be different from the preceding ones, would make great claims, would be a prophetic seer, would wear out the saints and would think to change times and laws.

The early Christians understood this prophecy and knew that out of the Roman Empire, the fourth beast; the man of sin would rise. Since this man of sin, the little horn in Daniel chapter 7, would wage war on the believers, Paul reached the conclusion that he would rise to power *before* the rapture of the saints at Jesus' second coming (2 Thessalonians 2:1-3). It all fits together!

JOHN'S PROPHECY OF THE NUMBER OF THE BEAST: 666 AND THE MARK OF THE BEAST.

Revelation chapter 13 mentions the *little horn* as a *beast* which represents the total fulfillment of Daniel and John's prophecies related to the one called the *man of sin* by Paul and the *Antichrist* by John.

Then I saw another beast coming up out of the earth, and he had two horns like a lamb and spoke like a dragon. And he exercises all the authority of the first beast in his presence, and causes the earth and those who dwell in it to worship the first beast, whose deadly wound was healed. He performs great signs, so that he even makes fire come down from heaven on the earth in the sight of men. And he deceives those who dwell on the earth by those signs which he was granted to do in the sight of the beast, telling those who dwell on the earth to make an image to the beast who was wounded by the sword and lived. He was granted power to give breath to the image of the beast, that the image of the beast should both speak and cause as many as would not worship the image of the beast to be killed. He causes all, both small and great, rich and poor, free and slave, to receive a mark on their right hand or on their foreheads, and that no one may buy or sell except one who has the mark or the name of the beast, or the number of his name. Here is wisdom. Let him who has understanding calculate the number of the beast, for it is the number of a man: His number is 666. Revelation 13:11-18

There is a reason why John did not identify the beast. John was writing while in exile from the Roman emperor in the isle of Patmos. The Church was suffering a severe and systematic persecution by Emperor Nero. In order to avoid any reprisals to the believers if the letter he was sending was intercepted by the Roman Authorities he writes in a secret language of symbolism sound used by the Jews and in the numerical value each letter had in the Hebrew alphabet. The pronunciation of the name Nero in Hebrew **Nrwn Qsr** is exactly 666.

The Beast of Revelation is the same beast of Daniel, referring to the Roman Empire and its emperor Nero. The pagan writer Apollonius of Tyana, a contemporary of Nero, specifically writes that Nero was called a "beast" due to his perverse and sadistic nature, feared and equally hated by the pagan Romans.

It is interesting to note that the letters of the Roman alphabet in the title borne by the Pope –*VICARIUS FILLI DEI*–, have a numerical meaning. Romans numbers are commonly used nowadays in different legal papers and writings. The I means 1; the V, 5; the X, 10; the L, 50; the C, 100 and the D, 500.

The total amount of the numerical alphabet here is 666: the number of the beast, which is a human number.

This key does not only apply to the Roman Empire; there are other keys in this strange mystery. The title of pope, taken by the Roman emperors as one of their names, comes from the Latin expression PATRIX PAX or "Father of Peace"; they considered themselves to be God's representatives on earth too. The title of pope in Latin –Papa– is made up by pa (from patrix) + pa (from pax).

The Greek letters in *LATEINOS (LATIN)*, the official language of the Roman Church, equals a total of 666 too according to the Greek numbers. L is 30, A is 1, T is 300, E is 5, I is 10, N is 50, O is 70 and S is 200. These numbers equals a total of 666.

We do not believe that every man who has held the position of Pope in the Roman Church, good or evil, is the beast of Revelation. We allude to the papal "system" derived from Babylonian paganism and followed by the Roman Empire.[5]

This key in Revelation gave great courage to the Christian Waldensians, who lived before Luther's Reformation, and later on to the followers of the Protestant Reformation. In chapter 19 of the last book of the Bible we find a warning for those who are

---

5   R. Woodrow, Babylon Mystery Religion, RWEA, p. 159-60

rooted in the Babylonian system. As we have already mentioned, one of the main items of the Reformation was that the papacy represented the Antichrist and Rome, the Babylon in Revelation 19.

Peter closes his second letter written from Rome like this: ***She who is in Babylon, elect together with you, greets you; and so does Mark my son (1 Peter 5:12).***

THE MARK OF THE BEAST

We have all heard about the computer in Switzerland which has the name of every inhabitant on earth. Or we have heard such things as the fact that many have had an electronic "chip" implanted which will be required by the Antichrist to be able to buy or sell; or that governments are planning to implant chips in newly-born babies so that they are able to receive the mark of the beast.

In Biblical symbolism a mark, or the engraving or a deep impression refers to a sign that identifies those who you pledge to follow. Usually the engraving is on the hand or the forehead symbolizing your labor and your mind. Throughout the Bible to have engraved or to have written on their hands or heads represents those you have become slaves or servants of. In the same way it is used of God's people (Deut. 6.8, Isa 49.16, Rev. 3.12, Rev 7.3, Rev 14.1, 14.4, Rev 22.4) It is also here used referring to those that submit to Caesar and the Roman state in order to obtain social respect and it's benefits (political, economic, Religious, etc.) ***Those that worship the beast whose names were not written in the lamb's book of life (Rev 13.8)***

The mark on the right hand or the forehead mentioned by John can also refer to the Catholic baptism representing faithfulness to the pope and the Roman system. During the times of the Medieval Inquisition and the conquest of the American continent, people needed to have been baptized into the Catholic Church in order to be able to buy or sell; those who were not baptized, rich or poor, young or old, free or slave– were persecuted and, in many cases, suffered martyrdom because of their faith.

As I teach on the subject and speak to many believers who ignore the meaning of this prophecies, I hear that their fear is that the government will force people to have the mark of the beast through some computer chip or otherwise and be condemned to eternal judgment as proposed by dispensationalist teachings.

God loves his people and wants to make them free from those mistakes derived from Babylonian idolatry which has spread all around the world.[6]

---

6   Ibíd. p. 161

CHAPTER
7

PAUL'S PROPHECY
– THE MAN OF SIN

*N*ow, brethren, concerning the coming of our Lord Jesus Christ and our gathering together to Him, we ask you, not to be soon shaken in mind or troubled, either by spirit or by word or by letter, as if from us, as though the day of Christ had come. Let no one deceive you by any means; for that Day will not come unless the falling away comes first, and the man of sin is revealed, the son of perdition, who opposes and exalts himself above all that is called God or that is worshiped, so that he sits as God in the temple of God, showing himself that he is God.*

2 Thessalonians 2:1-4

WANDERING AWAY FROM THE TRUE FAITH

When we study Paul's prophecy, we can see that he links the man of sin with a falling away: "… *for that Day will not come un-*

less the falling away comes first, and the man of sin is revealed, the son of perdition... (2 Tes. 2:3). The Greek Word used here is "apostasia", which is defined by Strong's Concordance as "defection from the truth". This would not be an apostasy from religion into atheism, but rather a falling away that would take place within the Christian church. As Lenski writes: *This is the apostasy. It is, therefore, to be sought in the Church visible and not outside the church, not in the pagan world, in the general moral decline, in Islam, in the French Revolution, in the rise and spread of Freemasonry, in Soviet Russia or in lesser phenomena.*[1]

Has this apostasy already taken place, or is it yet to happen in the future? Those who are familiar with the Church history know the answer.

The original New Testament Church was full of truth and spiritual power.

The original New Testament Church was full of truth and spiritual power, But as time went on, as the inspired apostles had warned under the inspiration of the Holy Spirit (Acts 20:29-30; 1 Timothy 4:1-3; 2 Peter 2:2-3), there began to be departures from the true faith. The mystery of iniquity was at work. They engaged in paganism and eventually the **Church**, with worldwide recognition during the fourth and fifth centuries, became the fallen Church. We find a historical and biblical explanation in Ralph Woodrow's book, *Babylon, Mystery Religion.*[2] The falling away could be a future event only if the Christian doctrines

---

1   [36] R:C:H: Lenski, The Interpretation of Saint Paul's Epistles, p.433.
2   [37] Ralph Woodrow, Babylon, Mystery Religion (Riverside, CA, Ralph Woodrow Evangelistic Association, Inc.,1966).

had remained unchanged throughout the centuries up to the present day. But this obviously has not been the case.

While the apostasy evolved, the bishop of Rome rose to power claiming to be the "Bishop of bishops"; he stated that the whole Christian world should look to him as *the head* and Rome as *the seat* of the Church. Over the centuries, this apostasy has continued with a **man** at Rome exalting himself above all others, demanding to be honored and worshipped, which is a constant reminder of the falling away occurred centuries ago.

Isaac Newton writes: *If the apostasy be rightly charged upon the Church of Rome, it follows that the man of sin is the pope; this doesn't mean a particular pope but the pope in general, as the chief head and supporter of this apostasy. The apostasy produces him and he promotes the apostasy.*[38] This is Barnes' explanation: *That his rise (the pope's) was preceded by a great apostasy, or departure from the purity of the simple gospel as revealed in the New Testament, cannot be reasonably doubted by anyone acquainted with the history of the Church. That he is the creation or result of that apostasy, is equally clear.* [4]

THE TEMPLE OF GOD: IN SEARCH OF A PLACE OF AUTHORITY

According to Paul's prophecy, the man of sin would '*exalt himself above all ... in the temple of God*' (2 Thessalonians 2:4). The futurists believe that Paul was referring to a future Jewish temple in Jerusalem. Unless this verse is an exception, Paul *never* used this expression to speak about the Jewish temple. Several times, he used in reference to the believers or the Church, but never to a literal building.

---

3   [38] Newton, op.cit., p.28
4   [39] Barnes, op.cit., p.1112.

Do you not know that you are the temple of God and that the Spirit of God dwells in you? If anyone defiles the temple of God, God will destroy him. For the temple of God is holy, which temple you are. 1 Corinthians 3:16-17

Or do you not know that your body is the temple of the Holy Spirit who is in you, whom you have from God, and you are not your own? 1 Corinthians 6:19

.. .you also, as living stones, are being built up a spiritual house... the church of the living God, the pillar and ground of the truth. 1 Peter 2:5; 1 Timothy 3:15

And what agreement has the temple of God with idols? For you are the temple of the living God. 2 Corinthians 6:16a

Now, therefore, you are no longer strangers and foreigners, but fellow citizens with the saints and members of the household of God, having been built on the foundation of the apostles and prophets, Jesus Christ Himself being the chief cornerstone, in whom the whole building, being fitted together, grows into a holy temple in the Lord, in whom you also are being built together for a dwelling place of God in the Spirit. Ephesians 2: 19-22

The temple of God is now the Church.

As Barnes points out, the "Christian Church" would be the kingdom where this man of sin would be established. He also says: *We don't have to understand this as the temple in Jerusalem... The idea is that the Antichrist would present himself in the midst of the Church as claiming the honors due to God alone... The authority claimed by the pope of Rome meets the full force of the language used here by the apostle.* [5]

The man of sin would 'sit' in the temple of God 'as God', implying he would claim a place of rulership within the Church.

The term "sit" *(kathizo)* refers to a "seat" *(kathedra)*, from which the word "cathedral" is derived, the bishop's seat. When the pope speaks "ex cathedra", he does it officially from his seat; his statements are considered infallible. Guinness writes: *There, in that exalted cathedral position, and claiming to represent God, the man of sin was to act and abide as the pretended vicar, but the real antagonist, of Christ, undermining His authority, abolishing His laws and oppressing His people.* [6]

In 2 Thessalonians 2:4 we read another description of the man of sin: ... *who opposes and exalts himself above all that is called God or that is worshipped, so that he sits as God in the temple of God, showing himself that he is God.* This means that the man of sin would exalt himself with great pride, would make great claims and magnify himself above all others.

We can find other similar expressions in other scriptures. The prince of Tyrus said: *I am God; I sit in the seat of God* (Ezequiel

---

5   [40] Ibid., p.1114.
6   [41] Guinness, op.cit., p.57.

28:2). The king of Babylon, full of pride, declared: *I will ascend into heaven, I will exalt my throne above the stars of God; (…) I will be like the Most High* (Isaiah 14:13-14). Daniel wrote about one who *shall exalt and magnify himself above every god (…) for he shall exalt himself above them all* (Daniel 11: 36-37).

We can see the pride and arrogance of the leaders who exalt and magnify themselves above every god and sit on the throne of God, as God. In the case of the man of sin, he would magnify himself above everyone in the Church! That is, he would not claim to be just "a" leader in the Church, but "the" leader of the Church. The man of sin would declare that he is like God and would magnify himself as the head of the Church, a position which belongs only to Christ, showing that he is God. There is no article before the word "God", which means that the man of sin would claim to have divine attributes. Barnes writes: *This expression doesn't imply that in fact he would claim to be the true God, but only that he sits in the temple and manifests himself 'as if' he were God. He claims such honors and such reverence as the true God would if He should appear in human form.*[7]

Have the popes claimed to be above all that is called God, have they claimed to be as God in the temple of God, and have they tried to show that they are divine? Yes they have! They claimed to be greater than all kings and emperors, and to reign not only on earth but also in heaven and in hell. They took for themselves attributes and titles which only belong to God. At the coronation of Pope Innocent X, these words were addressed to him by a cardinal kneeling before him: *"Most holy and blessed Father, head of the Church, ruler of the world, to whom the keys of the Kingdom of heaven have are committed, whom the angels in*

---

7   [42] Barnes, op.cit., p.1114

heaven revere, and the gates of hell fear and the whole world adores, we specially venerate, worship and adore thee!".

Moreri, a noted historian, writes: *"To make war against the pope is to make war against God, seeing the pope is God and God is the pope."* Decius declared: *"The pope can do all things that God can do."* Pope Leo XIII said about himself in 1890: *"The supreme teacher of the Church is the Roman Pontiff. Union of minds therefore requires, together with a perfect accord in the one faith, complete submission and obedience of will to the Church and to the Roman Pontiff, as to God himself."* In 1894 he said: *"We hold the place of Almighty God on earth."*

On April 30, 1922, on the throne of the Vatican and in the presence of a group of cardinals, bishops, priests and nuns who were bowing down before him, Pope Pius XI arrogantly declared: *"You know that I am the Holy Father, the representative of God on earth, the Vicar of Christ, which means that I am God on the earth".*

The pagan Caesar called himself "Our Lord and God". For many centuries the popes accepted the same title.

On the arches built in honor of Pope Borgia, we can read these words: *"Rome was great under Caesar; now she is greater: Alexander VI reigns. The former was a man, this is a god."* Pope Pius X, when he was the Archbishop of Venice, said: *"The Pope is not only the representative of Jesus Christ, he is Jesus Christ himself hidden under a veil of flesh and blood. Does the Pope speak? It is Jesus Christ who speaks."*

The following passage is an extract of the real words pronounced by the popes:

*The Roman pontiff judges all men, but he is judged by no one...
We declare... to be subject to the Roman pontiff is necessary for the
salvation of every creature. That which was said about Christ, "he
has subdued all things under his feet", can be verified in me... I
have the authority of the King of kings. I am all in all and above
all... I am able to do almost all things that God can do... Therefore,
if those things I do are said not to be done by a man but by God:
What can you do to me but God? Therefore, do not marvel if I have
the power to change times, to alter and abrogate laws, to dispense
with all things. Yes, with the precepts of Christ; because like Christ
forbade Peter to use the sword and exhorted his disciples not to use
any external force in revenge, so do not I, Pope Nicholas writing to
the French bishops, exhort them to draw out their material swords?
Therefore, as I began, so I conclude, commanding, declaring and
pronouncing that it is necessary for the salvation of every creature to
be subject to me.[8]*

FALSE SIGNS COVERING THE TRUTH OF A FALSE APOSTLE

Paul refers to the man of sin too as *the son of perdition* (2
Thessalonians 2:3). The same title is given to Judas Iscariot
(John 17:12). Through this double use of the term, the Holy
Spirit is apparently indicating that the man of perdition would
resemble Judas. Judas was in appearance a bishop and apostle
(Acts 1:20,25). Nevertheless, *he was a thief, and had the money
box; and he used to take what was put in it* (John 12:6). Such
words could be of use to describe the papal practices during the
Middle Ages also properly called the Dark Ages . Although Judas

---

8   [43] See John Foxe, *Acts and Monuments.*

had received thirty pieces of silver to betray Jesus, he went up to him in the garden, kissed him and said: *Greetings, Rabbi.* In the same way, the pope professes to be Christ's apostle and friend, but he has betrayed him by promoting teachings and traditions which are contrary to Jesus', such as indulgence selling, prayers for the dead, payment for masses, relic selling, offerings before idols, etc.

The rise to power of the man of sin would take place together with *all power, signs, and lying wonders* (2 Thessalonians 2:9). Volumes would be filled with a detailed account of all the miracles which have supposedly happened within this system: crucifixes have spoken; idols have sweated, moved their eyes and hands, opened their mouths, healed diseases, raised the dead, mended broken bones; souls form purgatory have appeared on deserted roads begging for masses to be said in their behalf; many have claimed that the Virgin Mary visited them, etc. All these miracles, whether real or faked, greatly increased the fallen Church.

The man of sin then, would appear in connection with the falling away; he would rise to power within the very system of the Christian Church, claiming to sit above all others, as God; his accession would be accompanied by signs and lying wonders. We have seen the detailed evidence that these things have found fulfillment with the papacy.

Some disagree to this interpretation due to Paul's words: *"the man of sin"* who, in their opinion, refers to an individual man and not to a succession of men. This is not necessarily true. "The" is used in the expression *the man of God* (2 Timothy 3:17), alluding to a type of men of a certain character, a succession of similar individuals. Or we read about the *High Priest* (Hebrews 9:7), which means a succession of high priests. Ephesians 2:15

refers to the Church –a long line or a succession of believers throughout the centuries– as *one new man*. Many times in the Scriptures a single beast represents a whole empire or kingdom, with all their changes and revolutions from beginning to end. The four beasts in Daniel 7 symbolize four kings, but their meaning is not limited to individual kings because each of these empires had a succession of rulers.

Grammatically, the expression "the man of sin" could be either an individual or a succession of similar individuals. There is a strong hint that it could refer to a succession of individuals. "He that rules" meant a succession of Caesars. For that reason, it would be correct to think that "he that sits" refers to a succession of men. However, this interpretation does not eliminate the idea of a single man because there is only one person occupying the papal office at any given time.

Here we must consider something else: the fact that the little horn *shall persecute the saints of the Most High (...) for a time and times and half a time* (Daniel 7:25). The early Christians, not knowing times or seasons (Acts 1:7), had no possibility to determine that the world would continue to exist for over 2,000 more years. From their perspective, they could have believed that the fall of the Roman empire would occur all of a sudden, the Antichrist would be an individual who would rise to power and prevail against the saints for a literal period of time of three years and a half. Several centuries later, when the Reformation shed light on the study of the prophecy, many Christians were able to see that these prophecies had been fulfilled, although it had been so over a period of time which was longer than they had originally expected.

Rome had fallen. But it was a decline and fall, which took place over a period of years. The rise of the Papacy was built over the years too; its rise was gradual. Many years passed before it met all the requirements of the prophecy. Scholars thought that the time, times and half a time –three years and a half or 1,260 days– during which the little horn would prevail against the saints, represented 1,260 years. It is a fact that the papacy wore out the saints century after century in the Middle Ages, when it is the belief that more than fifty million people were tortured and killed.

Prophecy is thought to be a wonderful combination of clarity and darkness.

There is plenty of evidence to show the hand of God, but not enough to make the readers become fatalists; plenty to prove that the message comes from God, but not enough to reveal all the details of its fulfillment. This has been the case of the prophecy about the man of sin.

CHAPTER
8

JOHN'S PROPHECY – THE SPIRIT OF THE ANTICHRIST

Little children, it is the last hour; and as you have heard that the Antichrist is coming, even now many antichrists have come, by which we know that it is the last hour. They went out from us, but they were not of us; for if they had been of us, they would have continued with us; but they went out that they might be made manifest, that none of them were of us.

–1 John 2:18-19

... and every spirit that does not confess that Jesus Christ has come in the flesh is not of God. And this is the spirit of the Antichrist, which you have heard was coming, and is now already in the world.–1 John 4:3

The real Antichrist

John is the only Bible author who uses the word "antichrist". During a time when there were many new teachings around, the apostle's aim was to help Christians keep the original faith they had inherited and been taught from the beginning.

That which was from the beginning, which we have heard, which we have seen with our eyes (…) This is the message which we have heard from Him and declare to you (1 John 1:1,5). He writes about the instruction they had had from the beginning which is the word they had heard *(1 John 2:7). Therefore let that abide in you which you heard from the beginning. If what you heard from the beginning abides in you, you also will abide in the Son and in the Father (2:24). For this is the message that you heard from the beginning… (3:11).* He mentions the commandment they had had from the beginning *(2 John 1:5-6);* and this is: *that we love one another.*

The reason why John specially emphasizes the expression "that you heard from the beginning" is that many people had abandoned the original faith to follow false teachings. He called them antichrists. *Little children (…) you have heard that the Antichrist is coming, even now many antichrists have come (…) they went out from us (1 John 2:18-19).*

These antichrists, a type of the Antichrist who was to come, were not atheists, but people who had confessed the Christian faith. We agree to the Scofield Bible's note: *"They went out from us" refers to their doctrine. No doubt, at that time like today those who deny the Son call themselves Christians.* If John said that those confessing the Christian faith, but following wrong teachings, were a type of the coming Antichrist, why should we try to find him outside the Christian realm? Even Scofield, at least in a note, wrote: *The "little horn" is an apostate not from Judaism but from Christianity.*[1] Let us have a look at this scripture about the Antichrist:

Who is a liar but he who denies that Jesus is the Christ? He is antichrist who denies the Father and the Son. Whoever denies the Son does not have the Father either; he who acknowledges the Son has the Father also. Therefore let that abide in you which you heard from the beginning. If what you heard from the beginning abides in you, you also will abide in the Son and in the Father. And this is the promise that He has promised us—eternal life. These things I have written to you concerning those who try to deceive you. 1 John 2:22-26:

Once again, he calls those who spread teachings in opposition to what they had heard from the beginning antichrists, because through these ideas they were denying the Father and the Son.

But this was not an open denial since John mentions how attractive these doctrines were. By reading the term "denied", some may assume that the Antichrist will be an atheist, a person who denies the existence of God, or at least who is unfaithful. We have heard that the Antichrist is *the number one atheist in the world*[2]; or that *the blasphemy of the little horn seems to be a bla-*

---

1   [45] Ibid., p.918
2   [46] Howard C. Estep. *Antichrist's Kingdom* (Colton, CA: World Prophetic Ministry), p. 24 (booklet)

tant act of unfaithfulness[3]47. However, the early Christians never heard about an unfaithful Antichrist. Apparently, this idea was first introduced in a commentary by Berengaud in the IX century.[4]

Apostle John uses this word to refer to those who were teaching false doctrines, which would be later known as Gnosticism; and also very likely to Judaizers that claimed to be Christians (1 John 2.22) for that reason, the purpose of his letters was to reveal false teachers' heresy and confirm the faith of true believers.

Apostle Joseph Mattera, Overseeing Bishop of Resurrection Church in Brooklyn, in the U.S., has recently written an article with the title *Identifying the Antichrist* where he suggests that the Antichrist is not an individual person, but a *spirit* teaching false doctrines.

I. In 1 John 2:18, Apostle John wrote that he was living in the last hour when the Antichrist would come.

   1. The "last hour" cannot obviously refer to the end of the world, more than 2,000 years later. Some try to explain this by saying that now we are living in the "last hour of the end times", which sounds more like a personal interpretation (eisegesis) than a correct objective interpretation of the Bible (exegesis).

   2. The careful study of other passages about the end times shows that Peter, Paul, John and others believed that they were all living in the last days (Acts 2:16-17, 1 John 2:18, 1 Peter 4:7, 2 Timothy 3:1, Judas 17-19, Revelation 1:1).

---

3   [47] V.K. Van De Venter, *Some Errors of Futurism* (booklet, 1936) quoting Maitland, p.8.

4   Guinness, op.cit. p. 125.

A. The only conclusion to all this is that the "last hour" did not refer to something which would take place thousands of years later; but to the "last days" of the Jewish Levitical system of animal sacrifices, and the "last days" for the Jewish nation which was going to be destroyed a generation after Jesus' death on the cross. Therefore this would be the official beginning of the new "age of the Kingdom" (Please read Matthew 24:34, Luke 9:27, Hebrews 12:27-28.). The apostles and the early Church were all Jewish believers who spoke about God's punishment over the nation of Israel due to their denial of Jesus as the Messiah.

B. The last days of Israel took place in the year 70 A.D., a generation after the Lord's death, when Jerusalem was besieged by the Roman army and the holy temple was desecrated. Luke 21:20 mentions the abomination of desolation.

II. Apostle John identifies the antichrists with those people who did not stay in the Church, and speaks about the "last hour" (Please read 1 John 2:18-19).

III. Apostle John also identifies the spirit of the antichrist, unleashed in the world; with those who do not confess that Jesus "has come in the flesh" (Please read 1 John 4:2-3).

   1. He was obviously referring to those who make the attempt to introduce the Platonic Gnosticism in the Church. Gnosticism, a heretical sect which did great harm to the Church in the early centuries, held the belief that the flesh is bad and only the spirit is good. They even taught that the god of the Old Testament was evil (the god of the flesh who created the natural world and needed animal sacrifices to be appeased; that the god of the New Testament was good and that

true Christianity means trying to get rid of the flesh to be able to live in the spirit.

IV. The antichrist is a false spirit which spreads wrong teachings in the Church; it is not a single person.

1. The term "antichrist" is never used in the book of Revelation or in any of the other letters, except 1 and 2 John. Nevertheless, their writers never refer to the Antichrist as a spirit of false teaching which rises to power and took Jesus' importance for himself, apart from the flesh or the natural kingdom.

V. A new type of Gnosticism has been filtering in the Church during the last 150 years.

1. The Church fled from the cities and found a kind of paradise in the surroundings or the rural areas.

2. The Church was focused on spiritual matters leaving behind the Reformation and cultural and social transformation; unlike Christians in the U.S. who founded most of the Ivy League universities with the purpose of training believers as well as guiding the nation in every walk of life.

3. The Evangelical Church embraced the escapist theology of dispensationalism, and is right now occupied in how to go to heaven and the rapture, instead of paying attention to the Lord's prayer in Matthew 6 where Jesus said that his will be done *on earth as in heaven.*

Fred Peters writes: *When we teach, just like reformers and Protestants did for 1,000 years, that the papacy –the dynasty of popes– is the Antichrist, many point out that the Antichrist should be an incredulous, atheistic and unfaithful person, while the Pope is nothing of the sort. This way they rule out with a single movement of their hand, the prophetic teaching that shook the papacy to its very foundations. More than once, an honest seeker asks a preacher whether the pope is the Antichrist of the Bible, and the matter is reduced to a one-minute reply in the most superficial way: "No, because he does not deny the Father and the Son"... and the subject is over because the seeker stops his seeking, unless he is determined to find out all the truth and the reason for this teaching of reformers and Protestants.*[5]

The antichrists mentioned by John were not atheists, but confessed Christians. Their teachings deceived some Christians leading them to accept false ideas. Atheism could never be so attractive, because it does not pretend to be a Christian doctrine. Therefore, what does it mean "that they denied the Father and the Son"? It does not mean that they denied the existence of God but they denied Him in other ways, especially by confessing their Christian faith and at the same time following false teachings which are contrary to the original message of the Church. This point is made clear when we look at the use of the word "to deny" in the Bible.

DENYING THE TRUTH

1. Jude, just like John, wrote about the apostasy which was beginning to appear in the Church:

    Beloved, while I was very diligent to write to you concerning our common salvation, I found it necessary to write to you exhorting you to contend earnestly for the faith which was once for all delivered to the saints. For certain men have crept in unnoticed, which long ago were marked out for this condemnation, ungodly men, who turn the

---

5   Fred Peters, op. cit., p.29

*grace of our God into lewdness and deny the only
Lord God and our Lord Jesus Christ. Jude 3-4*
(emphasis added by the author)

These false teachers' new ideas were so attractive that they
were covertly introduced. Through their wrong, false teachings
they *denied* the Lord. It cannot be proven that these apostates
denied the existence of God, because if they had done so, they
would not have been able to enter the scene this way.

In 2 Peter we read, too, about the apostasy that would arise
within the Church:

> *But there were also false prophets among the peo-
> ple, even as there will be false teachers among you,
> who will secretly bring in destructive heresies, even
> denying the Lord who bought them, and bring on
> themselves swift destruction. And many will fol-
> low their destructive ways, because of whom the
> way of truth will be blasphemed. 2 Peter 2:1-2*

It is evident that these false teachers did not deny the existence of God, because this would not have deceived the Christians to whom Peter wrote. They denied Christ through wrong,
deceitful teachings. On a previous occasion, Peter said that the
Jews had handed Jesus over and had *denied* him before Pilate:
*But you denied the Holy One and the Just (...) and killed the Prince
of life, whom God raised from the dead* (Acts 3:14-15). Those who
denied Christ did not deny his existence. They denied him because they rejected his words and crucified him.

1. Paul used the word "deny" in connection with those who
    shared false teachings among Christians. He calls them
    deceivers (...) who subvert whole households, teaching

things which they ought not, for the sake of dishonest gain. These people were not "spiritually healthy", but paid attention to Judaic tales and commandments which made men turn away from the truth. *They profess to know God, but in works they deny Him, being abominable, disobedient, and disqualified for every good work* **(Titus 1:16).**

It is obvious that the term "denied" in Peter, Paul and Judas's writing is not a synonym of atheism.

Those who denied the Lord by abandoning their original Christian faith were known as antichrists.

The following passage about the antichrists is in 1 John:

Beloved, do not believe every spirit, but test the spirits, whether they are of God; because many false prophets have gone out into the world. By this you know the Spirit of God: Every spirit that confesses that Jesus Christ has come in the flesh is of God, and every spirit that does not confess that Jesus Christ has come in the flesh is not of God. And this is the spirit of the Antichrist, which you have heard was coming, and is now already in the world (...) They are of the world (...) We are of God. He who knows God hears us; he who is not of God does not hear us. By this we know the spirit of truth and the spirit of error. 1 John 4:1-6:

So as John and the other apostles had received their message from Christ himself, they had the authority to declare that those who did not believe the message were not of God. Those who did not keep firm in the faith of the apostles were "false prophets"; their inspiration did not come from the Holy Spirit but from the spirit of the Antichrist. John did not write about such things as political corruption, alcoholism, prostitution, brutality or crime in the streets. Christians were able to recognize these things easily. John was referring to the deceit of false teachings.

John warned people, encouraging them to remain in the truth they had heard from the beginning –the apostolic doctrine–:

> *For many deceivers have gone out into the world who do not confess Jesus Christ as coming in the flesh. This is a deceiver and an antichrist. Look to yourselves, that we do not lose those things we worked for, but that we may receive a full reward. Whoever transgresses and does not abide in the doctrine of Christ does not have God. He who abides in the doctrine of Christ has both the Father and the Son. 2 John 7-9*

Any teaching which denies that Jesus Christ came in the flesh is not precisely a denial of his existence (because this would not deceive Christians). Apparently, it was a wrong, false view regarding his incarnation. Let us see these facts:

According to Irenaeus, the *Ebionites* taught that Christ was not born from a supernatural conception; they considered him to be only a human being. The *Gnostics* questioned the truth of Christ's human nature; they believed that the historical Christ was a veil of the true one: the heavenly Christ, not the one in the flesh. *Cerinthus'* followers believed that there was a difference between the heavenly Christ and Jesus of Nazareth, and that the two became temporarily one. The *Docetists* taught that the body of Christ was a ghost, instead of a man of flesh and blood. The *Theodocians* thought that Christ was only a man and had received his divinity at birth. The *Adoptionists* and *Paul of Samosata's* followers thought that Jesus had been born as a man, but he gained his divinity through his moral perfection.

Although all these groups shared false teachings about Christ's incarnation, they were not atheists. They were 'antichrists' as they turned away from the faith tat was taught 'at' the beginning. The fact that John mentioned specially a popular false idea at that time, that Jesus had not come in the flesh, is not an indication that the Antichrist would only deny the very teachings of those apostles. Neither the futurists nor those who believe that the prophecies have already had their fulfillment limit the errors of the Antichrist to this subject.

THE MEANING OF THE WORD "ANTICHRIST"

Some believe that John used the word "antichrist" to refer to a person who opposes Christ. Millions of people have opposed Christ. Paul himself, before his conversion, was Christ's opponent. Jews, pagans and members of non-Christian religions oppose Christ. The fact that John used the word "antichrists" to refer to the people who confessed the Christian faith, but were in opposition to Christ due to their false teachings, is a single point of identification. These antichrists were a type of the Antichrist who would come which clearly shows that he will present himself as a Christian, allegedly in favor of Christ, but in fact he will be against him through his false teachings.

It is well-known that the word "antichrist" can refer to:

(1) against (in opposition to) Christ;

(2) instead of (in the place of) Christ; or

(3) both meanings.

As Elliot has written: *When anti is combined with the noun which means an agent of any type, or an official, the compound word means a vice-official, or an official of the same kind who opposes, or sometimes both things.*[6]

We find an example of this word with both meanings in the terminology of the Roman Catholic Church. At times two men claimed to be the pope. He who was considered hostile, who substituted himself by occupying someone else's position, was called an "antipope". A man who professes to be the head of the Church and occupies the position that belongs to Christ, what else could he be but an Antichrist who is against the Lord? The reason is very simple: only Christ is the head of the Church (Ephesians 1:22; 4:15; 5:23; Colossians 1:18).

Porcelli says that the title held by the Pope, the Vicar of Christ, can only be translated as "antichristos" in Greek, that is the Vice-Christ, the substitute of Christ, or the Antichrist.[7] The popes have claimed a title for themselves which is the equivalent of the word coined by John.

OPPOSED TEACHINGS

Just like the "antichrists" mentioned by John, the popes have denied the Lord through the spreading of false teachings which make people turn away from the truth. They have even dared to

---

6   Elliott, op. cit, Vol. 1, pp.67, 68.
7   Porcelli, op. cit., p.72.

oppose Christ by sharing beliefs which are completely opposite to the message that Christ and the apostles taught.

1. *Prayer: And when you pray, do not use vain repetitions as the heathen do. For they think that they will be heard for their many words (Matthew 6:7).* Those who believe that the pope is the head of the Church say again and again prayers such as the Our Father, the Hail Mary, and the Glory is, etc. On praying the rosary, these prayers are repeated 53 times.

2. *Treasures. Do not lay up for yourselves treasures on earth, where moth and rust destroy and where thieves break in and steal.* The papal Church has done just the opposite. Let us have a look at all the riches and treasures in the Vatican. Some of the crowns worn by the popes are worth more than one million dollars. Many of the huge cathedrals and churches around the world are luxuriously decorated with silver and gold. In Latin America we have seen expensive cathedrals with idols and golden altars, while most of the poor live in clay huts nearby. If there is a system or a corporation which has built treasures on earth, in direct conflict with Jesus' teaching, it is the Roman Catholic Church.

3. *Love. But I tell you not to resist an evil person. But whoever slaps you on your right cheek, turn the other to him also. (...) love your enemies, bless those who curse you, do good to those who hate you, and pray for those who spitefully use you and persecute you (Matthew 5:39-44).* Unlike this, the Papacy fomented the terrible Inquisition in which Protestants were crushed as poisonous serpents. They used any methods at hand to torture those who did not accept the pope's sayings.

4. *Father. Do not call anyone on earth your father; for One is your Father, He who is in heaven (Matthew 23:9).* Although Jesus spoke against the use of religious titles, the members of the Catholic Church always use the title "father" when addressing a priest.

5. *Marriage. A bishop then must be blameless, the husband of one wife (1 Timothy 3:2).* The members of the New Testament Church, including Peter, were married (Matthew 8:14, 1 Corinthians 9:5). The early Church considered the teaching forbidding marriage a diabolical doctrine. But, as we know, for centuries the Roman Church has insisted on the celibacy of priests and nuns. This has led weak men to become sexual predators and child abusers, a common claim against the priesthood around the world today. In addition, many priests and nuns have left the Roman Catholic Church or the priesthood and turned to Protestant Churches for fellowship.

6. *Idols and images. ...keep yourselves from idols (1 John 5:21).* Do the members of the Papal Church obey this commandment? No! The Catholic Church promotes and encourages the use of idols and images on house walls, on car dashboards, in churches, in roadside shrines and, above all, around its members' necks. The early Church never had images of Christ, Mary or the saints in its worship.

7. *The Scriptures.* The Bible praises those who study the Scriptures (Acts 17:11) but the Roman Catholic Church was against the reading of the Word for many centuries. Pope Pius IV said: "The Bible is not for the people; he who wishes to be saved should renounce it. It is a forbidden book. Bible societies are satanic inventions".

John's Prophecy – The Spirit of the Antichrist   139

In 860 Pope Nicholas I forbade the reading of the Bible, and also Gregory VII in 1073. In 1198, Innocent III issued a decree forbidding either the possession or reading of the Bible; the famous Council of Trent did the same. Pius VII denounced the Bibles as "plagues" in 1816. Gregory XVI condemned the biblical societies in 1844 and ordered priests to destroy all the Bibles they could find.

Jorge Mario Bergolio the recently elected Pope Francis 1 has recently declared that "Only the Roman Catholic Church is able to properly interpret the Scriptures" thus adopting the medieval ages position of the Vatican.

We believe all this shows without any question that although the Papacy claims to represent Christ, it has definitely opposed Him. In Daniel, Paul and John's writings we can see the following facts:

1. As to time, the man of sin would appear when repression was suppressed. We have examined the reasons that lead us to believe that this repression refers to the Roman empire and when it fell, the papacy rose to power.

2. As to place, the man of sin would rise to power where the Caesar had been removed: that is Rome. It would be a Roman power.

3. As to religion, the man of sin would exalt himself above all others in the Church, not only as a leader but also as "the" leader or the head of the Church. This way, he would be in Christ's place and against him: Antichrist.

According to the Bible, the Spirit of Antichrist would be a "Roman" power that would exalt itself above all others in the fallen Church.

If we combine these two words, we make the expression: Roman Church. History has proven that the apostasy took place in Rome. We only need to ask which man became the head of this system, and we will have identified the man of sin!

Although not every detail was clear at once, over the years it was proven that the Papacy became a persecuting power which wore out the saints of the Most High, spoke blasphemous words and carried out those things foreseen by the prophecies about the Antichrist.

Froom writes: *In the centuries before the Reformation, a number of pious people began to express their conviction that the terrible prophecies about the Antichrist were in the process of fulfillment; they felt that the falling away had already taken place. They declared that the Antichrist was already seated at the churchly temple of God, clothed in purple and scarlet.*[8]

CHRONICLES OF MARTYRS AND REFORMERS

Eberhard II, Archbishop of Salzburg (1200-1246), taught that the little horn of Daniel 7 was the Pope who was a wolf in sheep's clothing, the Antichrist, the son of perdition. He did not expect the coming of an unidentified individual antichrist. Instead looking back over the centuries, he saw the historical Papacy as a succession or system of antichrists risen after the fall of Rome, the fulfillment of the prophecies about the Antichrist. He was excommunicated by the Pope and died under the ban in 1246.[9]

John Foxe, the author of the famous book *Foxe's Book of Martyrs* gives a list of learned men between 1331 and 1360 who

---

8   Froom, op. cit., Vol.2, p.66.
9   Ibid., Vol 1, p.798

contended against the Pope's false claims. One of them, Michael of Cesena, who had many followers, some of which were slain, declared that the Pope was the Antichrist and the Church of Rome was the whore of Babylon, drunk with the blood of the saints.[10]

John Wycliffe the renowned English reformer, taught that Daniel's persecuting little horn had been fulfilled with the Papacy, which arose out of the fourth kingdom: Rome. "Why is it necessary in unbelief to look for another Antichrist? he asked." Daniel chapter 7 describes the Antichrist as a horn arising in the time of the fourth kingdom... *wearing out the saints of the Most High*".[11] His book, *The Mirror of Antichrist* is filled with references to the Pope as the Antichrist.

Hundreds of thousands of English Lollards were Wycliffe's followers. We share their testimony in the words of one of them, Lord Cobban. When he was brought before King Henry V and demanded to be subject to the Pope like an obedient child, Coban replied: "As for the Pope and his spirituality, I owe him neither loyalty nor service, for as much as I know him by the scriptures to be the great Antichrist, the son of perdition".[12] This happened a century before Martin Luther.

Walter Brute, a noted scholar, prophetic expositor and a follower of Wycliffe, was accused in 1391 of having declared many times that "the Pope is the Antichrist and a seducer of the people".[13]

Sir John Oldcastle (1360-1417), famous Christian of Hertfordshire, spoke about the Pope in these words: "I know

---

10   Fox, op.cit. p.445.
11   Froom, op. cit., Vol. 2, p.55
12   Guinness, op. cit., p. 134.
13   Foxe, op. cit. Vol.1, p.543.

him by the Scriptures to be the great Antichrist, the son of perdition… Rome is the very nest of the Antichrist, and out of the nest come out all the disciples of him". Because of this, he was sentenced to death. Although the sentence was not carried out speedily, in 1417 he was taken to St Giles, suspended in chains and slowly burned to death while his voice ascended to God in praise.[14]

John Huss (1369-1415), born in Bohemia, was a well educated man who was influenced by Wycliffe's writings and that made him break with the Roman Church. He labeled the Pope as the Antichrist of whom the Bible had warned. His writings constantly refer to the Antichrist as the enemy of the Church, not as a Jew, pagan or Turk, but as a false confessor of the name of Christ. Pope Martin V issued a bull in 1418 where he ordered the punishment of the people who stood firm in Wycliffe and Huss' teachings. Sixty miles from Prague, on a high mountain the city of Tabor was built to which the "Hussites" could flee from the Antichrist.[15]

Huss was condemned as a heretic and passed over to the secular authorities for his execution. Surrounded by a guard of one thousand armed men and a vast crowd of spectators, he was led through the church yard from where he saw a bonfire of his books at the public square. While he was praying on his knees, they tied his hands behind his back and bound his neck with a rusty chain. They piled up straw and wood around him. His name means "goose" in the Bohemian language and it is said that at the place of his execution Huss said: "This day ye are burning a *goose*, but from my ashes will arise a *swan* which ye will not be able to roast", an expression later quoted by Luther. "Huss

---

14   Ibid. pp. 636-641.
15   Froom. Op. cit., Vol. 2, P.121.

began to sing", writes Froom, "but the wind swept the flames into his face and silenced his words. Only his lips moved until they were stilled in death for his stand against the Antichrist of Bible prophecy!".[16]

Martin Luther (1483-1546), disagreed with the sale of indulgences while he was still a priest in the Roman Catholic Church. At first, he sought a reform within the Church. But as he grew in the knowledge of Christ, he saw that a reformation would not be possible and that the message was "come out of her". Once free from the domination of this system, he began to consider the possibility of the Pope as the Antichrist. Eventually, he made up his mind to believe that he was.

Luther's friends, in fear for his personal safety, begged him to suppress his book *To the German Nobility*. This was his reply to this on August 18, 1520: "We here are of the conviction that the Papacy is the seat of the true and real Antichrist... personally I owe the Pope no other obedience than that to Antichrist".[17] Two months later his book *On the Babylonian Captivity of the Church* was published. He wrote about the Papacy (the system, not an individual Pope) as "nothing else than the kingdom of Babylon and of very Antichrist ... For who is the man of sin and the son of perdition, but the one who by his teaching and his ordinances increases the sin and perdition of souls in the Church while he yet sits in the church as if he were God? All these conditions have now for many ages been fulfilled by the papal tyranny".[18]

In 1540 Luther wrote: "Oh Christ, my Lord, look down upon us and bring upon us thy day of Judgment and destroy the brood of Satan in Rome. There sits the man of whom Apostle

---

16 [60] Ibid. p.116.

17 Ibid. p.256.

18 Martin Luther, First Principles, pp. 196,197

Paul wrote (2 Thessalonians 2:3-4) that he will oppose and exalt himself above all that is called God, that man of sin, that son of perdition who suppresses the law of God and exalts his commandments above the commandments of God".[19]

According to Luther, the Bible does not describe the Antichrist as an infidel, or a super-politician but as one who would rise within the church realm, that is, "in the midst of Christendom". Concerning the man of sin, he pointed out that "he does not sit in a stable of fiends or a swine sty or in a company of infidels but in the highest and holiest place of all: in the temple of God....Is not this to sit in the temple of God and profess to be the Ruler in the whole Church? What is the temple of God? Is it a temple made of stones and wood? Did not Paul say *for the temple of God is holy, which temple you are*? What is it to sit but to rule, to teach and to judge? Who from the beginning of the Church has dared to call himself the ruler of all the Church but the Pope? None of the saints, none of the heretics ever uttered so horrible a word of pride".[20]

It is clear that Luther did not believe that the Antichrist would be an individual person at the end of the age because he declared: "The Antichrist, of whom Paul speaks, now reigns at the court of Rome." As the *Encyclopedia Britannica* states, "these ideas became the dynamic force that drove Luther in his contest with the Papacy".[21]

Philipp Melanchthon (1497-1560), who worked in partnership with Luther also, identified the Antichrist in this way: "Since it is certain that the pontiffs and monks have forbidden marriage (see 1 Timothy 4:1-3), it is most manifest,

19 Froom, op. cit., Vol. 2, p.281.
20 [64] Luther, Works, Vol. 2, p.385.
21 [65] Encyclopedia Britannica, Article: "Antichrist", Vol. 2, p. 61.

and true without any doubt that the Roman pontiff, with his whole order and kingdom is very Antichrist… Likewise, in 2 Thessalonians Paul clearly says that the man of sin will rule in the Church, exalting himself above the worship to God".[22]

The French reformer **John Calvin** (1509-1564) is generally considered as second in influence, only to Luther. Originally a son of the Papal Church, he embraced the Protestant faith in 1532. His published works filled about fifty volumes. As to the Pope, he wrote: "I deny him to be the Vicar of Christ, who in furiously persecuting the gospel demonstrates by his conduct that he is the Antichrist; I deny that he is the successor of Peter… I deny him to be the head of the Church".[23]

In his classic work *Institutes* he wrote: "Some people think us too severe and censorious when we call the Roman pontiff Antichrist. But those who are of this opinion do not consider that they bring the same charge of presumption gainst Paul himself, after whom we speak and whose language we adopt… I shall briefly show that Paul's words (2 Thessalonians 2) are not capable of *any other interpretation* than that which applies them to the Papacy". Then he points out that the Antichrist would conceal himself under the character of the church, 'as wearing a mask', and that the Papacy had fulfilled the characteristics set forth by Paul.

John Knox (1505-1572), famous for his reformation work in Scotland, was persecuted from country to country until the Scottish government was in the hands of Protestants. He preached on the abolishing of the Roman traditions and ceremonies as well as of "the tyranny the Pope had exerted over the Church for so many centuries." And that he should be acknowleged as the

22 [68] Ibid. p. 288.
23 Calvin, Tracts, Vol. 1, pp.219, 220.

very "Antichrist, the son of perdition of whom Paul speaks".[24] In a public document Knox said: "As for the Roman Church, as it is now corrupted, I have no doubt that this is the synagogue of Satan; and its head, who is called the Pope, is the man of sin of whom the apostle speaks".

Huldreich Zwingli (1484-1531), was an prominent figure in the work of the reformation that broke out in Switzerland. On December 28, 1524, he declared that the papacy was evil and had to be overthrown by preaching the Word with love and never with hatred: "I know that in it works the might and power of the devil that is , of the Antichrist... the Papacy has to be abolished, but there is not a better way to do it than through the Word of God (2 Thessalonians 2) because as soon as the world receives it in the correct way, it will turn away from the Pope without compulsion".[25]

William Tyndale (1484-1536), the first translator of the Bible from Greek into English, reformer and martyr, believed that the Papal Church was Babylon and that the Pope was the man of sin, the Antichrist seated in the temple of God, which is the Church. To confirm this fact, he repeatedly cited 2 Thessalonians.[26]

Years later (in 1611), the translators of the King James Bible version identified the Papacy as the man of sin and noticed the fact that the publishing of the biblical truth was dealing a greta blow to him. Therefore, they wrote this dedication to the king: "The zeal of Your Majesty toward the house of God does not slack or go backward but is more and more kindled, manifesting itself to all Christendom by writing in defence of the truth, *which has given such a blow on to the man of sin* as will

---

24   Knox, the Zurich Letters, p. 199.
25   Principal Works of Zwingli, Vol. 7, p.135.
26   Ibid., p.356

not be healed". It is evident that these men did not believe that the man of sin was an individual person who would manifest himself in the future!

King James (1566-1625) believed that the reign of the Antichrist began after the removal of the Roman emperors. This was, of course, a reference to the rise of the Papacy which, in his opinion, was the Antichrist and the mystery of lawlessness.[27]

Thomas Cranmer (1489-1556) wrote these words about the Papacy in 1550: "I know the Antichrist has obscured the glory of God, and the true knowledge of his Word, covering them in mist and clouds of error and ignorance through false interpretations… The Roman Antichrist has exalted himself above other bishops as the vicar of God, or rather as God himself; he has taken for himself authority over kings and emperors and sits in the temple of God, that is in the consciences of men which make them respect his decrees more than God's laws; and for money he abolishes God's laws… giving men permission to break them".[28] After quoting the prophecies in the books of Daniel and Revelation, he said: "It is logical to conclude that Rome is the throne of the Antichrist, and that the Pope is the true Antichrist. I could prove all this through many other scriptures, old writers and strong reasons".[29]

During his final testimony, he spoke of the Pope as the Antichrist and after saying a few more words, he was led to the bonfire that made him a blackened corpse.

Sir Isaac Newton (1642-1727) is well-known due to his scientific research on gravitation. He was a writer, mathematician, philosopher and student of the biblical prophecy. His *Observations*

27 Ibid. pp.540, 541.
28 Cranmer, Works, Vol. 1, pp. 6, 7.
29 Ibid. pp.62, 63.

Upon the prophecies of Daniel and The Apocalypse of St. John was published six years after his death. Newton linked the little horn in Daniel with the Papacy, which rose among the ten kingdoms emerged from the Roman empire. "But this kingdom was different from the other ten... With its eyes, it could foresee things; with its mouth, it spoke great words and changed times and laws. It was a prophet and also a king. Such a seer, prophet and king is the Church of Rome. A seer, a bishop in the literal meaning of the word; and so this church claims the universal bishopric. With his mouth, he gives laws to kings and nations as an oracle, he pretends to be infallible and that his decrees are binding for the whole world; this makes him a prophet of the highest rank".[30]

John Wesley (1703-1791), founder of Methodism, whose ministry has affected the lives of multiplied thousands, believed that the prophecies about the Antichrist, the man of sin "had their fulfillment in the Roman Papacy".[31] In 1754 Wesley wrote these words concerning the Papacy: "He is in an emphatical sense the man of sin, as he increases all manner of sin above measure.. He is also rightly called the Son of Perdition, as he has caused the death of numberless multitudes, both of his opposers and followers... He it is that exalts himself above all that is called God or that is worshipped, claiming the highest power and honor and claiming all the prerogatives which belong to God alone".[32]

Froom sus up the evidence in these words: "We have seen the remarkable unanimity of belief of Reformation leaders in every land, that the Antichrist of prophecy is not to be a single

---

30 [88] Sir Isaac Newton, *Observations Upon the Prophecies* (London: 1831 edition). P.75.
31 [89] Wesley, *Explanatory Notes Upon the New Testament*, pp.290.
32 [90] Quoted by Albert Close, *Antichrist and His Ten Kingdoms* (London: Thynne and Company, 1917), and p.110.

individual, some sort of superman, who will wreck the world before the second coming of Christ. Instead they found that it was a vast system of apostasy or rather, an imposing counterfeit of truth which had been developed within the jurisdiction of the divinely appointed custodian of truth: the Christian Church".[33]

In the centuries after the Reformation important books about the Papal Antichrist were written. We will mention two of them: *Roman Antichrist*, written by Andreas Helwig of Berlin in 1612 (the first according to Froom as well as Elliot to link the number 666 with the Papal designation "Vicarius Filii Dei"); and *Dissertations on the Prophecies*, written by Thomas Newton in 1748, which shows that the prophecy about the man of sin has been fulfilled in the Roman Papacy.

This same point of view was emphasized in the Protestant creed. *The Westminster Confession of Faith* used by the Church of England and later by the Presbyterian Church says (Chapter 25, Section 6):

> *There is no other Head of the Church but the Lord Jesus Christ. Nor can the Pope of Rome, in any sense, be head thereof; but is that Antichrist, that man of sin, and Son of Perdition, that exalts himself, in the Church, against Christ and all that is called God.*

This same basic declaration can be found in *The Savoy Declaration* of the Congregational Church, *The Baptist Confession* of 1689, and *The Philadelphia Confession of faith*. *The Moreland confession* of 1508 and 1535 (which represented the beliefs of the Waldensians Brethren) says in its 8th article:

---

33 [91] Froom, op., cit., Vol.2, P.793.

> *That Antichrist, the man of sin, doth sit in the temple of God, that is, in the Church; of whom the prophets and Christ and his apostles foretold, admonishing all the godly, to beware of him and his errors, and not to be drawn aside from the truth.*

In 1536 the reformation work in Switzerland produced *The Helvetic Confession*, which called the Papacy "the predicted Antichrist." The Lutheran statement contained in the *Smalcald Articles* says: *"The Pope is the very Antichrist, who exalts himself above Christ and opposes him, because he will not permit Christians be saved without his power, which, nevertheless, is nothing, and is neither ordained nor commanded by God".*

The Protestant churches established in America shared the same view about the Papacy. In 1680 the churches of New England drew up a confession of faith which declared that Jesus Christ is the head of the Church and not the Pope of Rome, who is in fact the Antichrist. Froom writes: *"This was the commonly accepted American position".*[34] As Samuel Lee (1625-1691), a learned minister of New Bristol, Rhode Island said: *"It is agreed among all maintainers of the Evangelical Church that the Roman Pontiff is the Antichrist".*[35]

Jonathan Edwards (1703-1758), a famous revivalist and third president of Princeton University, identified the "Pope and his clergy" as the power prophesized in 2 Thessalonians 2 and other scriptures. His grandson, **Timothy Dwight** (1752-1817), a minister too, spoke of how the Popes *"have seated themselves in the church or temple of God, and claimed to be God by assuming the powers which belong only to God: for instance, powers of making laws to bind the consciences of men; or pardoning sin; or forming*

---

34 Ibid. Vol. 3, p.111.
35 Lee, The Cittong Off of Antichrist, p. 1.

religious establishments; or introducing new laws for the conduct and government of the church… Thus have they exalted themselves above all that is called God or that is worshipped".[36]

THE FOUNDATIONS OF OUR FAITH

After many pages, carefully documented to prove his statements, Froom concludes: *"The futurist view of an individual Antichrist was unknown among the Protestants in North America prior to the nineteenth century".[37]* However, today many Christians have only heard about the futurist ideas. They are not even aware that another interpretation exists.

As we have mentioned before, these were the three great truths preached in the sermons that began the Protestant reformation:

(1) By Scripture alone. The Bible is the only resource for "all" Christian doctrines.

(2) The just shall live by faith and this is only by grace. (Not through the works of Romanism).

(3) The papacy is the Antichrist of the Bible. This was a message "for" Christ and "against" the Antichrist.

Froom writes: "The whole Reformation was based on this testimony".[38]

Hundreds of books were written in a confrontation between Protestant and Catholic pens regarding the subject of Antichrist. It was such a big clash, that in 1516 the Fifth Lutheran Council ordered not to write or preach a single word about the Antichrist. Nevertheless, in Germany, Switzerland,

---

36 Dwight, A Sermon Preached at Northampton, p.27.
37 Froom, op., cit., Vol.3, p.257.
38 Ibid. Vol, 2, p.243.

England, France, Denmark and Sweden, the ministers of several Protestant churches continued to preach this message with power and conviction. The Bible was reaching the common people. Thousands had come to recognize thePapacy as the Anrichrist, a teaching wich dealt havoc to the church of Rome.

Thousands recognized the papacy as the Antichrist, a teaching which created havoc in the Church of Rome.

We have a challenge before us: to accept the beliefs and teachings of the patriarchs and reformers of the Church, or to accept the ideas of Dispensationalism or Futurism which is the legacy of the Roman Catholic counter-reformation.

I understand the controversy this can provoke these days, because the Church has lost its prophetic voice to silence the voices of its critics through it, but as I heard a man of God say many years ago: *I prefer being alone and walking in the truth to being wrong in the company of many.* John the Baptist lost his head for declaring the truth about Herod's condition.

The apostle Paul exhorts us to know the times we are living in, to awake out of sleep, to cast off the works of darkness and put on the armor of light (Romans 13:11-12).

PART 4

THE COMING OF CHRIST

Chapter 9

DANIEL'S
SEVENTY WEEKS

Seventy weeks are determined for *your people and for your holy city*, to finish the transgression, to make an end of sins, to make reconciliation for iniquity, to bring in everlasting righteousness, to seal up vision and prophecy, and to anoint the Most Holy. Know therefore and understand, that from the going forth of the command to restore and build Jerusalem *until Messiah the Prince*, there shall be seven weeks and sixty-two weeks; the street shall be built again, and the wall, even in troublesome times. And after the sixty-two weeks Messiah shall be cut off, but not for Himself; and the people of *the prince* who is to come *shall destroy the city and the sanctuary*. The end of it shall be with a flood, and till the end of the war desolations are determined. Then he shall confirm a *covenant with many for one week; but in the middle of the week he shall*

> *bring an end to sacrifice and offering. And on the*
> *wing of abominations shall be one who makes*
> *desolate, even until the consummation, which*
> *is determined, is poured out on the desolate.–*
> *Daniel 9:24-27 Emphasis by the author*

PROPHETIC INTERPRETATIONS, RIGHT AND WRONG.

This wonderful prophecy about the people of Daniel and the city of Jerusalem is related to a seventy-week period. Bible scholars believe that these seventy weeks, or 490 days, symbolize years; each day represents one year, which is 490 years.

In Numbers 14:34 the same principle is used. The people of Israel had to wander in the wilderness for forty years because of their unbelief, one year for each day that the spies were exploring the Promised Land. Likewise, we find this comparison in Ezekiel 4:6: I have laid on you a day for each year.

Christians agree on the fact that seven weeks and sixty-two weeks, that is sixty-nine weeks, equal 483 years until the coming of the Messiah; however, futurism and historicism have two interpretations which are totally different about the last week: the seventieth week.

The futurist interpretation says that there is a space or period of more than 2,000 years dividing the seventieth week from the other sixty-nine which point toward the arrival of the Messiah in reference, according to them, to the "second" coming and not the first one. The historical interpretation, on the contrary, says that there is no division at all between the last two weeks; the logical sequence is a whole period of seventy weeks.

According to dispensationalism or futurism the seventieth week is a period within which the Antichrist will make a covenant with the Jewish people. This covenant will allow them to make sacrifices in a temple rebuilt in Jerusalem during these seven years; but at the end of three and a half years, he will break the covenant stopping the sacrifices. For historicism, the last week refers to Christ and what happened three and a half years after his death, as the last and final sacrifice (Hebrews 9:26-27).

What a tremendous difference! Some believe this week will be in the future; others that it has already taken place! One interpretation says that there is a space of thousands of years between the sixty-ninth and seventieth weeks; the other one says that there is no space at all between these two weeks. One contends that the week refers to the Antichrist; the other that it is about Christ's ministry and the first years of the early Church. Such big differences can only mean that one of these two interpretations is wrong.

Like other authors, I believe that the historical interpretation is the correct one. The sixty-ninth week ends with the baptism of the Messiah in the waters of the Jordan by John the Baptist, and the beginning of the ministry of Jesus. In the middle of this week, after three and a half years, the Messiah was killed; being a perfect sacrifice, it became the last one and stopped all the others. We read in Daniel book: ...but in the middle of the week he shall bring an end to sacrifice and offering (priestly). And on the wing of abominations (the siege of Jerusalem, the persecution of Jews, the destruction of the temple, etc.) shall be one who makes desolate... (the Roman army). Some interpret this as the period of Antiochus Epiphanes and the Maccabean Revolt, but the time measuring "and the classical interpretation method does not exclude the fact that the main aspects of this prophetic message were fulfilled in Jesus Christ, the destruction of the temple and the destruction of Jerusalem. Daniel's language has a distinct eschatological character at times, which leads to a fulfillment of the prophecy in different levels". [1]

THE FULFILLMENT OF THE PROPHECY

Let us have a detailed look at all the basic aspects of the seventy weeks and their literal fulfillment:

The seventy weeks or seventy times seven years, is a term associated with the people of Daniel, the Jews and the holy city of Jerusalem. By comparing Daniel 7:25 to Revelation 11: 2-3, 12:6-14 and 13:5 we can establish that the week of years (490) is made of years of 360 days.

The week calculation begins with Artaxerxes' order to restore Jerusalem in 445 B.C. The period is chronologically divided into:

Seven times seven: forty-nine years; from 445 to 396 B.C. from the decree to Nehemiah's arrival and the celebration of the renewal of the covenant in Jerusalem.

Seventy-two times seven: 434 years; from 396 to 32 A.D. from the dedication of the second temple to the anointing of our Lord Jesus Christ in the waters of the Jordan River.

One time seven years[2]: From then on, the first three years and a half were the time of the ministry of Jesus Christ; in the middle of this period of seven years the Lord's sacrifice on the cross takes place.

As St. Augustine wrote: Daniel even defined the time when Christ would come and suffer with the exact date.[3]

---

1   Spirit Filled Bible, Thomas Nelson PublishersP1051
2   Ibid.
3   The Prophetic Faith of our Fathers, Vol. 1, pg. 487.

Eusebius writes: Thus the whole period of Jesus Christ's teachings and miracles took three years and a half, which is half a week. In his gospel, John the evangelist makes this very clear for those who are attentive.[4]

Jesus Christ was the perfect sacrifice. In God's eyes, the old system of continual sacrifices came to an end on Mount Calvary.

The reintroduction of the sacrifices in the temple 2,000 years after the death of the Savior is a return to the old covenant but Hebrews declares: …where there is remission of these (sins), there is no longer an offering for sin (Hebrews 10:18). In v. 26 we read: …there no longer remains a sacrifice for sins.

For some years after the crucifixion, the Jews continued to offer their sacrifices, but God did not accept them.

This shows the real meaning of certain passages in the New Testament which define in a similar way a set time when Christ would die. For example:

> *Therefore they sought to take Him; but no one laid a hand on Him, because His hour had not yet come. John 7:30*

> *Then Jesus said to them: 'My time has not yet come, but your time is always ready'. John 7:6*

Just before his betrayal and death, Jesus said:

---

4   Eusebius, The Proof of the Gospel, book 8, chap. 2

My time is at hand. Matthew 26:18

Behold, the hour is at hand... Matthew 26:45

Father, the hour has come. John 17:1

These and other Bible verses clearly indicate that there was a set time for the death of Jesus Christ. He came to fulfill the Scriptures and there is only one passage in the Old Testament that prophesied his death. This was Daniel's prophecy that the Messiah would be cut off in the middle of the week, at the end of his three-and-a-half-year ministry. This word had its "perfect" fulfillment.

What can be said then about the second three and a half days of the week? Daniel 9:27 declares that he would confirm a covenant with many. After the resurrection of Jesus, the disciples continued to preach exclusively to the Jews for three years and a half. The obvious reason is that although they had been sent to preach the gospel to every creature around the world, without knowing, they were fulfilling the period prophesied by Daniel for Israel.

Having this in mind, we are able to understand the following scriptures in their prophetic context:

> *... To the Jew first and also for the Greek. Romans 1:16 (emphasis added by the author)*

> *You (Israel) are sons of the prophets, and of the covenant which God made with our fathers (...) to you first...*

> *Acts 3:25-26 (emphasis added by the author)*

*It was necessary that the word of God should be
spoken to you first... Acts 13:46 (emphasis added
by the author)*

In the real sense of the word, the ministry of the disciples
was an extension of the ministry of Christ. This has continued
to the present day.

---

*You and I continue to take and share the
ministry of Christ.*

Adam Clarke writes in his Bible commentary: This prophecy
as a whole with its own times and events has been fulfilled to the
last word.[5]

In our studies about the seventy weeks in Daniel, we have seen
that there is neither mention of the Antichrist nor indication of
a covenant with the Jews he would make and break. In the next
chapters, we will analyze in detail the second coming of Christ
and the rapture or catching up. Paul declared that Jesus would
not come until the falling away took place and the man of sin,
the son of perdition, were revealed; until what was restraining the
lawless one were taken out of the way (2 Thessalonians 2:1-12).

The interpretation of this prophecy by individuals who have not
paid attention or examined the biblical context, has led many into
error. Let us remember, with fear and trembling, Apostle Peter's ad-
monition regarding the Bible, the relative importance of its words
and the proper place of the Scriptures. On interpreting the Bible,
we should pay attention to the context as well as to its full contents.

5   Clarke's Bible Commentary, notes on Daniel 9

The past, the present and the future depend on the Word of God.

And so we have the prophetic word confirmed, which you do well to heed as a light that shines in a dark place, until the day dawns and the morning star rises in your hearts; knowing this first, that <u>no prophecy of Scripture is of any private interpretation</u>, for prophecy never came by the will of man, but holy men of God spoke as they were moved by the Holy Spirit. 2 Peter 1:19-21 (emphasis added by the author)

Other versions say:

> *... No prophecy in Scripture ever came from the prophet's own understanding... (New Living Translation).*

> *... None of us can explain by ourselves a prophecy in the Scriptures. (Good News Translation).*

> *No prophecy of Scripture comes from one's own interpretation... (Holman Christian Standard Bible)*

Therefore, according to Peter's advice, the only way of interpreting the prophecies is searching through the whole Word of God for their meaning.

10

THE RAPTURE
- PART 1

WILL CHRIST COME IN TWO STAGES?

For this we say to you by the word of the Lord, that we who are alive and remain until the coming of the Lord will by no means precede those who are asleep. For the Lord Himself will descend from heaven with a shout, with the voice of an archangel, and with the trumpet of God. And the dead in Christ will rise first. Then we who are alive and remain shall be caught up together with them in the clouds <u>to meet the Lord in the air</u>. And thus we shall always be with the Lord. Therefore comfort one another with these words.–1 Thessalonians 4:15-18 (emphasis by the author)

> *But the day of the Lord will come as a thief in the*
> *night, in which the heavens will pass away with a*
> *great noise, and the elements will melt with fer-*
> *vent heat; both the earth and the works that are*
> *in it will be burned up.–2 Peter 3:10*

FACT OR FICTION?

In his book *Great Prophecies of the Bible*, Ralph Woodrow wrote almost entirely, the following two chapters which have been reproduced with the author's personal permission.

Nowadays, we hear a lot about the "rapture", which is preached and taught on Christian radio and television programs. "The ultimate journey", as some people call it, has been the plot of sensational movies. We can see bumper stickers with slogans such as: "In case of the rapture, this vehicle will have no driver"; or "The rapture: the only way to fly".

Dramatic sermons explain how thousands of people will suddenly disappear. There will be accidents where cars will veer off the road and fall over a cliff, while their drivers are raptured away. Planes will crash as Christian pilots go up in the rapture. Television programs will be interrupted for frantic voices to repot such things as: "A horrified husband says that he and his wife were having dinner, when she disappeared all of a sudden right in front of his eyes"; "a mother reports seeing her baby disappear from the crib"; "a Christian doctor who had just made the incision for a major surgery, suddenly disappeared through the ceiling of the operation room". Newspapers men will shout headlines on the "millions of people missing". Church members (those who were not raptured) will have emergency meetings to elect new leaders for the years ahead. The rapture has taken place! The Lord's trumpet has sounded! And life goes on... Is this the biblical description of the rapture?

THE END OR A NEW BEGINNING?

We can search all through the Bible and we will never find the word "rapture".

This comes from the Latin *rapere*, which is also the root of the word "rape" and means "seize" or "take away". It would be easier to share what the Bible says: "We will be caught up to meet the Lord in the air". Nevertheless, the word "rapture" is now a common term which applies to the catching up of the believers to meet the Lord, and for that reason we will use it here.

The word "rapture" is not what really matters. Neither the doctrine of the second coming of Christ, which has been the blessed hope of the Church throughout the centuries, nor the fact that believers will be caught up to meet the Lord in the air is the issue. The issue to consider here is if this rapture is a separate event prior to the coming of the Lord.

Christians who believe in the dispensationalist interpretation of prophecy teach that the second coming of Christ will be in two stages: first, the rapture (his coming *for* the saints); and later the revelation (his coming *with* the saints). They say that the interval between these two events, the period of the great tribulation takes seven years. Scriptures such as Revelation 1:7: *Behold, He is coming with clouds, and every eye will see Him* are applied to the revelation: his coming in power and glory. The rapture, on the other hand, is a quiet, invisible and secret coming. The following commentaries show this point of view:

His appearance in the clouds will be veiled to the human eye and no one will see him. He will appear and slip away: he will come for his jewels and slip away as under the cover of night.[1]

Quickly and invisibly, unperceived by the world, the Lord will come as a thief in the night and will catch up his waiting saints.[2]

(The rapture) will be a secret appearance and only the believers will know about it.[3]

In the rapture, only Christians will see him. It is a mystery, a "secret".[4]

It will be a secret, quiet, noiseless rapture which will be as sudden as the steps of a thief in the night. The world will only know that crowds have gone at the same time.[5]

With all respect for the sincere Christians who believe this, this is a strange idea for us. The text on which the rapture is based on means exactly the opposite!

> *For the Lord Himself will descend from heaven with a shout, with the voice of an archangel, and with the trumpet of God. And the dead in Christ will rise first. Then we who are alive and remain shall be caught up together with them in the clouds to meet the Lord in the air. 1 Thessalonians 4:16-17*

1   Oral Roberts, How to be Personally Prepared for the Second Coming of Christ (Tulsa: Oral Roberts Evangelistic Association, 1967) p. 34.
2   Jesse F. Silver, The Lord's Return (New York: Revell, 1914), p.260.
3   Herschel W. Ford, Seven Simple Sermons on the Second Coming (Grand Rapids: Zondervan Publishing House, 1970), p.143.
4   Hal Lindsey, The Late Great Planet Earth (Grand Rapids: Zondervan Publishing House, 1970), p.143.
5   G.S. Bishop, The Doctrine of Grace, p.341.

In our opinion, this text shows anything except a quiet, secret rapture. Amid the sound of the Lord himself descending from heaven, the voice of the archangel and the trumpet of God, we will hear the praise and rejoicing of huge crowds that will be caught up to meet Jesus!

Let us suppose that the Bible declared: "The Lord invisibly will descend from heaven, quietly." What would we reply to somebody who tells us this means He will come visibly and loudly? Would we not think that this twisting of words is a wrong doctrine? Now, if we turn this around, the Bible actually says: *The Lord himself will descend from heaven with a shout.* Reading "invisibly "or "quietly" in this description is just as wrong. If Paul had the intention to describe a secret event, then he chose the wrong words!

In fact, Jesus warned us against the idea of a secret second coming:

> *Then if anyone says to you: 'Look, here is the Christ!' or 'There!' do not believe it. Therefore if they say to you... 'Look, He is in the inner rooms!' do not believe it. For as the lightning comes from the east and flashes to the west, so also will the coming of the Son of Man be. Matthew 24:23-27*

There is no indication in the Bible that the second coming of Christ will be a secret event; only when it will take place remains a secret.

Jesus said several times that men did not know the day or the hour of the second coming. It will be "as in the days of Noah" when they were eating, drinking and getting married and did not expect destruction to come. ... *they (...) did not know until the flood came and took them all away, so also will the coming of the Son of Man be (Matthew 24:36-39)*. Unbelievers did not understand until the flood came; but when it finally happened, everybody understood. It was not a secret event! It was seen by those who believed and those who did not believe.

As a thief in the night

> *But concerning the times and the seasons, brethren, you have no need that I should write to you. For you yourselves know perfectly that the day of the Lord so comes as a thief in the night. For when they say: "Peace and safety!" then sudden destruction comes upon them, as labor pains upon a pregnant woman. 1 Thessalonians 5:1-3*

> *But know this, that if the master of the house had known what hour the thief would come, he would have watched and not allowed his house to be broken into. Therefore you also be ready, for the Son of Man is coming at an hour you do not expect. Matthew 24:43-44*

The coming of Christ will be like that of a thief in the sense that we do not know when it will occur. There is no indication here of a secret coming, in which He will take believers out of this world so that nobody will know what happened to them or who took them. We should not think of the Lord as a thief who works in the dark, for fear of being caught. This is the meaning: He will appear as a thief, but will not act like a thief!

Those who mock perhaps will ask: "Where is the promise of his coming?" But Peter assures us that the day of the Lord will come. We do not know when, however *the day of the Lord will come as a thief in the night (2 Peter 3:10)*. But once again, it says that it will not be a quiet event, because Peter relates it to a great noise: *...the day of the Lord will come as a thief in the night; in which the heavens will pass away with a great noise!*

In the famous rapture passage, after speaking about the coming of the Lord with a shout, Paul explains that we do not know *when* this will be, because that day will come as a thief in the night. ***But concerning the times and the seasons, brethren, you have no need that I should write to you. For you yourselves know perfectly that the day of the Lord so comes as a thief in the night (1 Thessalonians 5:1-2).*** What is misunderstood or hidden here? A coming of Christ as a secret event is just not possible. The context describes it as glorious, open and loudly. Only the day and hour are not revealed.

VICTORY AMID SUFFERING

Shortly before his death, Jesus told his disciples these words: ***In the world you will have tribulation (John 16:33).*** In the next verses we can read the prayer Jesus said for his disciples: ***I do not pray that You should take them out of the world, but that You should keep them from the evil one (John 17:15).***

Despite witnessing for Christ would not be easy as they would be persecuted and have suffering in this world, Jesus did not ask the Father to take the Church out of the world. The Church would stay in the world but would not be a part of it.

Some might say, however, that Jesus was praying only for the disciples at that time. This is far from the truth! ***I do not pray for*** *these alone, but also for those who will believe in Me through their word* (v. 20). Does that not include us too? Have we not believed in Christ as a result of the message that reached us from the early disciples? Of course we have! For that reason, Jesus was praying also for us. His prayer was that God would keep us from evil, because in this world we were going to suffer!

Let us suppose that Jesus had told the believers: "In the world you will have suffering… but I will pray that you be taken out of the world." If Jesus had said this prayer, those who teach about rapture before the tribulation would have a foundation for their position and, no doubt, would mention this statement to prove this. But since this verse says just the opposite, this must be evidence against the idea of a special "secret" coming to take the Church out of the world.

UNTIL THE VERY END

Instead of a Church being taken out of the world, Jesus taught that it would stay to fulfill a special purpose: the preaching of the gospel.

This is Jesus' command to his disciples: *Go therefore and make disciples of all the nations, baptizing them in the name of the Father and of the Son and of the Holy Spirit...* And he promised them: ... *and lo, I am with you always, even to the end of the age* (*aino*: age) *(Matthew 28: 19-20).*

How long will the Church be in the world fulfilling God's command? This mission will continue until the very end of the world. This promise would be strange if God's plan were to catch up the Church seven years before that time! Such promise would be meaningless if by the end of the world, the Church had already been taken out of the earth.

In previous chapters of the book of Matthew, Jesus taught the same. He shared a parable about a man who sowed good seed in his field; but then the enemy came and sowed tares among the wheat. Before this situation, the owner ordered *First gather together the tares and bind them in bundles to burn them, but gather the wheat into my barn (Matthew 13:24-30).*

There is no need to guess which is the correct meaning of the parable because Jesus explained it: the good seed –the wheat– is sowed by "the Son of Man": Jesus Christ. The tares –the children of the wicked one– are sowed by the enemy: the devil. Both things are sowed in the same field –*the world*–, where they grow together until the harvest. *The harvest is the end of the age... (Matthew 13:37-39).*

Therefore as the tares are gathered and burned in the fire, so it will be at the end of this age. The Son of Man will send out His angels, and they will gather out of His kingdom all things that offend, and those who practice lawlessness, and will cast them into the furnace of fire. There will be wailing and gnashing of teeth. Then the righteous will shine forth as the sun in the kingdom of their Father. Matthew 13: 40-43

Undoubtedly, the time of the division of the wicked and the righteous is at the end times.

Jesus said that "both" would grow "together" until "the end of the world", and then there would be a harvest to produce the great division. This is what the Bible teaches us. But for a rapture before the tribulation to make sense, it should say that they will not grow together in the field until the end of the world because it is taught that the wheat will be gathered earlier and separated from the tares, seven years before the end!

According to a note in the Scofield Reference Bible, *at the end of this age (v. 40) the tares are gathered and burn in the fire, but first the wheat is gathered in the barn.*[6] But if something comes first, this would be the judgment of the wicked, because in the parable we read: ***First gather together the tares and bind them in bundles to burn them**, but gather the wheat into my barn* (emphasis added by the author). This scripture says: "first the tares". The note in the Scofield Bible mentions just the opposite! Such twisting of words does not speak well of the pre-tribulation.

> *Immediately after the tribulation of those days the sun will be darkened, and the moon will not give its light; the stars will fall from heaven, and the powers of the heavens will be shaken. Then the sign of the Son of Man will appear in heaven, and then all the tribes of the earth will mourn, and they will see the Son of Man coming on the clouds of heaven with power and great glory. And He will send His angels with a great sound of a trumpet, and they will gather together His elect from the four winds, from one end of heaven to the other. Matthew 24:29-31*

> *Then two men will be in the field: one will be taken and the other left. Two women will be grinding at the mill: one will be taken and the other left. Watch therefore, for you do not know what*

---

6   C.I. Scofield, Scofield Reference Bible (New York: Oxford University Press, 1917), P. 1016.

hour your Lord is coming. But know this, that if the master of the house had known what hour the thief would come, he would have watched and not allowed his house to be broken into. Therefore you also be ready, for the Son of Man is coming at an hour you do not expect. Matthew 24:40-44

A deeper examination shows that Jesus compared the Kingdom to a net cast into the sea. It caught fish of every kind, some good, and other bad. At the end, the good ones were gathered into vessels and the bad ones were thrown away. When will this great separation take place? *So it will be at the end of the age. The angels will come forth, separate the wicked from among the just, and cast them into the furnace of fire (Matthew 13: 47-50).*

Jesus also compared the time of his coming with the days of Lot:

Likewise as it was also in the days of Lot: They ate, they drank, they bought, they sold, they planted, they built; but on the day that Lot went out of Sodom it rained fire and brimstone from heaven and destroyed them all. Even so will it be in the day when the Son of Man is revealed. Luke 17:28-30

Lot, who was an old testament believer, was saved from the fire and destruction; but those who did not believe were destroyed. Likewise, when Christ comes the believers will be caught up to receive the Lord in the air; while at the same time on that day, a destruction of fire and brimstone will bring on the world. There is no indication in this passage that Lot went out of Sodom and, seven years later, a burning destruction fell upon them. These things happened on the same day.

Jesus also compared his second coming with the destruction of the flood in the days of Noah: *They ate, they drank, they married wives, they were given in marriage, until the day that Noah entered the ark, and the flood came and destroyed them all (Luke 17.27). ... so also will the coming of the Son of Man be. Then two men will be in the field: one will be taken and the other left (Matthew 24:39-40).*

ONE: TAKEN, THE OTHER: LEFT

Many sermons have been preached about the fact that "one will be taken and the other will be left", with the meaning that Christians would be caught up in the rapture and unbelievers would stay on earth to go through the tribulation. But this cannot be correct because, according to this passage, unbelievers were destroyed by the flood. In the days of Noah, unbelievers *...did not know until the flood came and took them all away, so also will the coming of the Son of Man be. Then two men will be in the field: one will be taken and the other left. Two women will be grinding at the mill: one will be taken and the other left (Matthew 24:39-41).*

If we pay attention to the context, we understand that unbelievers will be surprised by death, by *sudden destruction* which will come with the Lord on his return (1 Thessalonians 5:3). The lives of those who have put their faith in Christ will be saved. They will indeed be rescued, *"caught up"*, above the sudden destruction, but this does not seem to be the focus of the passage.

Despite the world had already been destroyed by water, Peter wrote that the destruction to come upon the world in the future will be by fire: *... by which the world that then existed perished, being flooded with water. But the heavens and the* *earth which are now preserved by the same word, are reserved for fire until the day of judgment and perdition of ungodly men (2 Peter 3:6-7).*

Peter had heard with his own ears Jesus' promise: ... *I will come again and receive you to Myself... (John 14:3).* Years went by and mockers began to ask: "Where is the promise of his coming?" Peter replied in these words:

> *The Lord is not slack concerning His promise (...) the day of the Lord will come (...) in which the heavens will pass away with a great noise, and the elements will melt with fervent heat; both the earth and the works that are in it will be burned up (...) all these things will be dissolved. 2 Peter 3:9-11* (emphasis added by the author).

This is the way he described what Jesus had called "the end of the world". Some believe that this description refers to the literal end of this planet. Others, that the correct interpretation is the end of the age, and not necessarily the end of our planet. In the days of Noah, it is pointed out that "the existing world at that time perished", but the planet remained; likewise, "the existing heaven and earth now", this century, could end while the planet remains. However, "the end of the world" here refers to a definite end. There is no indication that the time will continue for seven more years after this. In our opinion, the song author was right when he wrote: "When the Lord' trumpet sounds, time will no longer exist..."

Peter continues to say:

> *Therefore, since all these things will be dissolved, what manner of persons ought you to be in holy*

conduct and godliness, looking for and hastening
the coming of the day of God, because of which
the heavens will be dissolved, being on fire, and
the elements will melt with fervent heat? 2 Peter
3:11-12

It is evident that Peter did not believe that Christians would
be taken out of the world seven years before the end. Why would
he encourage them to expect the coming of the Lord when
heaven passed away? Why would he speak about the end if his
real hope were an event occurred seven years before?

According to Peter, "the coming of the Lord" the day of
the Lord which will come "as a thief in the night" is the hour
when the heavens will pass away and the earth will be melted
with fervent heat. And according to Paul, "the day of the Lord",
which will come "as a thief in the night" (the same expression),
is the time of the rapture.

> *For the Lord Himself will descend from heaven*
> *(…) Then we who are alive and remain shall be*
> *caught up together with them in the clouds to meet*
> *the Lord in the air. And thus we shall always be*
> *with the Lord. But concerning the times and the*
> *seasons, brethren, you have no need that I should*
> *write to you. For you yourselves know perfectly*
> *that the day of the Lord so comes as a thief in the*
> *night. For when they say: "Peace and safety!" then*
> *sudden destruction comes upon them, as labor*
> *pains upon a pregnant woman. And they shall not*
> *escape. 1 Thessalonians 4:16-17 & 5:1-3*

Although this passage continues in the next chapter, it introduces a single idea. There is no indication that the rapture will be an event separated from the destruction coming upon the earth, at the end of the world.

HEAVEN AND EARTH WILL PASS AWAY

Jesus explained the aim of that day in these words: ***Heaven and earth will pass away (…) But of that day and hour no one knows, not even the angels of heaven, but My Father only (…) Watch therefore, for you do not know what hour your Lord is coming (Matthew 24:35-42).***

If Christians must "watch" over that day –when heaven and earth will pass away– it is clear that they will not be taken seven years later.

Job himself meant that the resurrection would not take place until heavens had passed away: ***But man dies and is laid away; indeed he breathes his last and where is he? (…) So man lies down and does not rise. Till the heavens are no more, they will not awake nor be roused from their sleep (Job 14:10-12).*** Such expressions as "till the heavens are no more", or "the heavens will pass away with a great noise" seem to show the real end of all things as we know them. Until then, the dead will not rise again.

Martha believed that Lazarus would rise again *in the resurrection at the last day (John 11:24)*. This was not a simple conclusion of hers, because Jesus referred several times to the resurrection as *the last day (John 6:39-40,44,54)*. Therefore the catching up or rapture happens at the same time that the resurrection of the dead in Christ (1 Thessalonians 4:16-17). It is evident that the rapture does not take place seven years before but on the last day.

The chapter on the resurrection (1 Corinthians 15) says that these things will happen ... *at the last trumpet. For the trumpet will sound, and the dead will be raised incorruptible, and we shall be changed (vv. 51-52).* We also know that on this "last day", at "the last trumpet", "the last enemy" will be destroyed. Paul declares: *The last enemy that will be destroyed is death (1 Corinthians 15:26).*

It will happen ... *in a moment, in the twinkling of an eye, at the last trumpet. For the trumpet will sound, and the dead will be raised.* Then in the resurrection and the rapture ... *shall be brought to pass the saying that is written: 'Death is swallowed up in victory' (vv. 52-54).* According to Dispensationalism, this takes place before the tribulation and after that seven more years come. But, what happens with those people who will be killed after that, some of whom will become martyrs for Christ? This interpretation requires another resurrection for them at the end of the tribulation. But if we place the destruction of the last enemy on the "last day", just as the Bible does, the last enemy is still the same.

What happens with the martyrs of the tribulation? John saw people who refused to worship the beast and were beheaded. But ... *they lived and reigned with Christ for a thousand years (...) This is the first resurrection. Blessed and holy is he who has part in the first resurrection (Revelation 20:4-6).* According to Dispensationalism, these people will be raised at the end of the period of tribulation. Therefore, the resurrection takes place during the rapture; both groups agree to this. Now, if the rapture occurs before the tribulation, how could the resurrection of the martyrs of the tribulation be *the first resurrection?* But, if the first resurrection is a bodily resurrection before the tribulation, the martyrs of the tribulation will be raised before being tortured. By placing the resurrection at the end, as the Bible does, we see that the Word of God makes sense. Regardless of our interpretation of Revelation 20:4-6, if the martyrs lived in the first centuries, in the Middle Ages or in the last years of this age, all of them would be included in the final resurrection with no need for additions to the Word.

Until the introduction of the doctrine of a secret rapture (of a relatively recent origin), the idea of being saved after the coming of the Lord would have been very strange! The Church never taught such a thing in the first eighteen centuries of its history!

Throughout the centuries preachers have been faithful to declare the teachings of Jesus and his disciples: be sober and vigilant to be ready for the coming of the Lord.

Peter thought that the apparent delay in the coming of the Lord was due to his desire that no one should die without coming to repentance (2 Peter 3:9). He obviously did not believe that people could be saved after the coming of the Lord!

Can you possibly imagine millions of people being saved after the coming of the Lord (the rapture)? This has never been the historical position of the Church. But nowadays, some churches have announced an addition to their statutes: legal news passing from the church leaders to the sinners. They believe that they will repent and be saved after the coming of the Lord in the rapture. Should anyone have doubts about the Christian faith, they will be certain of it after witnessing millions go missing. Those who are not gone in the rapture will have to call for urgent meetings to elect new leaders who can continue with the church work.

A DIFFERENT PLAN OF SALVATION?

Some people think that after the rapture, before the tribulation, God will have a different plan of salvation. As an author says: "Now we are saved by the blood of Christ but after the rapture, people will have to shed their own blood to be saved. It will be a road of martyrs to get to heaven!" Another one suggests that at that moment people will be saved or lost, according to the treatment they give to the Jews. I have a flyer with these words: "If you are left behind when Jesus comes, do not persecute the Jews, help them in their suffering. Because that can be your salvation; those who have protected and looked after the Jews, those who have given them refuge, food and clothes will be worthy of going into the age of the Kingdom".

This idea is apparently based on Jesus' words in the parable of the sheep and the goats. Jesus will tell the righteous –the sheep– that they gave him food, they gave him drink, he was a stranger and they took him in and visited him in prison. They will ask when they saw him in these circumstances; his answer will be: *Assuredly, I say to you, inasmuch as you did it to one of the least of these My brethren, you did it to Me (Matthew 25:40).*

The dispensationalist belief that "my brethren" means the Jews during the tribulation introduces a third kind of people in the parable; apart from the sheep or the righteous as "my brethren." There is no difference at all if Jesus had said: "My brethren, because you did it to one of the least: the hungry, the thirsty, the sick, and the oppressed". The proof of this is evident because the word "brethren" is only used when Jesus was speaking to the sheep. When he was addressing the goats, the word "brethren" is missing, as it is shown in the following parallel:

TO THE SHEEP

... inasmuch as you did it to one of the least of these My brethren, you did it to Me (Matthew 25:40).

TO THE GOATS

... inasmuch as you did not do it to one of the least of these, you did not do it to Me (Matthew 25:45).

After reading the whole passage, the idea becomes obvious. If the phrase "my brethren" means a different type of people instead of a simple way to address the sheep, it should have appeared also in the second part. Besides, Christ's "brethren" could not mean only a group of Jews, because Jesus himself said (recorded by Matthew) that *... whoever does the will of My Father in heaven is My brother and sister... (Matthew 12:50).* This is a relation on the basis of "grace", not a "race".

WHAT DAY AND HOUR?

Once and again, the Bible points out that the coming of the Lord will happen all of a sudden, that no man knows the day or the hour of the end of the world. If the rapture is an event which will take place seven years before the end, thousands of people could establish the exact date. They would only have to count seven years from the immediate disappearance of all babies and Christians.

Should there be any doubt, a ride to the cemetery would be the absolute proof that the rapture has occurred. If the corpses of true Christians a pious grandmother, a devoted minister or a recently deceased baby– were exhumed and empty coffins were found, it would be evident that the resurrection has already taken place. Sooner than later thousands of people would hear about this and they would be able to calculate the exact date of the end of the world. But as the Bible teaches, since no man knows the day or the hour of the end it is clear that the rapture is not a separate event which occurs seven years before the end.

Jesus' description of his coming rules out the idea of two separate events: *For the Son of Man will come in the glory of His Father with His angels, and then He will reward each according to his works (Matthew 16:27).* This cannot be a secret return of Christ on his own because he comes in glory with the angels; in this same hour, man will be rewarded. This does not match up with the idea of a previous rapture because if so many would have already been caught up and rewarded!

For whoever is ashamed of Me and My words in this adulterous and sinful generation, of him the Son of Man also will be ashamed when He comes in the glory of His Father with the holy angels (Mark 8:38). If Christ had come alone before, in a secret rapture, and had been ashamed of people, that would have already happened. Why, then, would he speak about these things in relation to his coming in glory with the angels?

The Christians of Thessaloniki were suffering "persecutions and tribulations" and the unbelievers afflicted them (2 Thessalonians 1:4-7). But Paul encouraged them with the truth: *... and to give you who are troubled rest with us when the Lord Jesus is revealed from heaven with His mighty angels, in flaming fire taking vengeance on those who do not know God, and on those who do not obey the gospel of our Lord Jesus Christ (...) when He comes, in that Day, to be glorified in His saints (2 Thessalonians 1:7-10).*

In this passage –like in the others– the reward for the righteous and the destruction that will fall upon the wicked are mixed regarding the time; both events take place on the coming of the Lord. We also see that when Jesus comes to save the suffering saints, he will appear in flaming fire to punish those who do not know God. The time He will be glorified in his saints is also the time of destruction, which will fall upon the wicked. There is no seven-year lapse between both events.

TWO STAGES OF A SECOND COMING?

Ralph Woodrow's study of the Bible, including prophecy, started at an early age. When he was young, just like the Bereans, he longed to *search the Scriptures daily to find out whether these things were so (Acts 17:11)*. Most of the Christians he knew at that time had been influenced by the dispensationalist interpretation of the prophecy that Jesus would come back twice; the first time in the secret rapture and seven years later, with glory and power at the end of the world. He knew that Jesus had come the first time and that *He will appear a second time, apart from sin, for salvation (Hebrews 9:28)*. But, where did the Bible teach about a third coming of Christ? Most people, of course, did not use the expression "the third coming"; they preferred to mention "two stages" of the second coming.

This idea seemed strange to me, like an addition to justify a theory. If the rapture were a stage separated from the coming of Christ with power and glory, one may wonder: how can each stage be a part of the second coming? If they are different events separated by several years, a coming following the second one would be a third coming. The Word never mention a third coming or "comings" in plural, and the phrase "two second comings" sounds contradictory.

In an attempt to explain this difficulty, some dispensationalist authors have even discussed the fact that "the rapture is not at all the second coming". One of them writes: *In fact, the rapture is not the second coming. The second coming is the visible, local and bodily appearance of Christ in the clouds of heaven while He is returning to the earth... in power and great glory*[7] Another one says: *The exciting event that will mark the end of the age of grace and open the door for the great tribulation is the rapture... in fact, "this is not the second coming of Christ" but the rapture or catching up of the true Church.*[8]

The attempt to turn the catching up into a separate event before the coming of Christ is completely opposite to the Word of God.

Jesus declared: ***Therefore you also be ready, for the Son of Man is coming at an hour you do not expect (Matthew 24:44).*** Why would Jesus recommend being ready for the "coming" of the Son of Man, if the rapture were to occur *before* his coming?

Jesus said: *Do business till I come (Luke 19:13).* How can the Church do business till He comes, if it will be caught up seven years before his coming? Jesus also promised: *I will come again and receive you to Myself.* Indeed, it is when Jesus comes that his people will be received to him. This reception does not take place seven years before his coming!

In perfect accord with Jesus' teachings, we read this exhortation to the disciples: *Therefore be patient, brethren, until the coming of the Lord... For yet a little while, and He who is coming will*

---

7   Frank M. Boyd, Ages and Dispensations *Springfield: Gospel Publishing Company
8   William W.Orr, Antichrist, Armageddon, and the End of the World (Grand Rapids: Dunham Publishing Company, 1966), p. 9

come (*James 5:7, Hebrews 10:37*). Once again, why encouraging Christians to be patient until the "coming" of the Lord, if their true hope were a rapture *before* his coming?

According to Paul, Christians are ... *eagerly waiting for the revelation of our Lord Jesus Christ (1 Corinthians 1:7).* If he had believed that they would be caught up to heaven in a secret rapture, seven years before the coming of the Lord, why did he not say that they were waiting for that? Undoubtedly, Paul did not believe that the rapture was a separate event. In the passage about the "rapture", he declares that the catching up of believers is *"the coming of the Lord" (1 Thessalonians 4:15).* In view of these things, we believe that these authors make an effort to explain that the rapture is not the coming of the Lord.

THE MEANING OF THE GREEK WORDS

Which is the meaning of the Greek words used to describe the second coming? An author says: ***Both phases of the second coming can be clearly distinguished in Greek. The "parousia"... is his coming "for" the saints... the "apokalupsis" (to reveal, to remove the veil, to make manifest) is his coming "with" his saints.*** [9] But, as we will see next, instead of indicating two separate events, these Greek words are actually used in an interchangeable way.

This is a list of the six Greek terms used to describe the second coming of Christ, their specific meaning and a Bible verse where each word appears:

1. ***Parousia*** (the personal presence of he who comes or arrives): *...be patient... until the coming of the Lord (James 5:7).*

---

9   Carl Sabiers, Where are the Dead? pp. 123,124.

2. ***Apokalupsis*** (the appearance, the revelation): ... *when the Lord Jesus is revealed from heaven with His mighty angels (2 Thessalonians 1:7).*

3. ***Epiphaneia*** (manifestation, glory): ... *our Lord Jesus Christ's appearing (1 Timothy 6:14).*

4. ***Phaneroo*** (to become apparent): ... *when He is revealed, we shall be like Him (1 John 3:2).*

5. ***Erchomai*** (the act of coming, to go from one place to another): *Do business till I come (Luke 19:13).*

6. ***Heko*** (the point of arrival): ... *hold fast what you have till I come (Revelation 2:25).*

The first word on our list, *parousia,* emphasizes the real personal presence of he who has come and arrived. There is no indication of a secret in this term. It was of common use when Paul spoke about the coming (parousia) of Titus (2 Corinthians 7:6); the coming (parousia) of Stephanas (1 Corinthians 16:17); and his own coming (parousia) to Philippi (Philippians 1:26).

Paul used this word in the famous passage about the rapture where "the coming (parousia) of the Lord" is mentioned, when Christians will be caught up to meet the Lord in the air (1 Thessalonians 4:15-17). But Paul's use of this word here cannot mean an event separated from the coming of the Lord at the end of the world, because in his second letter to the Thessalonians, he puts the *parousia* "after" the reign of the man of sin. In reference to "the coming of our Lord" and "our gathering together to him", Paul writes: ... **whom the Lord will consume with the breath of His mouth and destroy with the brightness of His coming (2 Thessalonians 2:8).**

Peter, like Paul, wrote about the "coming (parousia) of the Lord" at the end of the world when "the heavens will pass away with a great noise, and the elements will melt with fervent heat". He encouraged Christians by saying: *... **looking for and hastening the coming (parousia) of the day of God, because of which the heavens will be dissolved, being on fire, and the elements will melt with fervent heat (2 Peter 3:12).*** In both cases *parousia* cannot mean a rapture before the tribulation.

The plural form of the word *parousia* here has no relation with the coming of the Lord. The use of the definite article is correct, because it is not *a* coming but *the* coming of the Lord.

Peter told Christians: ... *rest your hope fully upon the grace that is to be brought to you at the revelation of Jesus Christ* (apokalupsis) (1 Peter 1:13). Those who teach that Christ comes first in the rapture and then the manifestation seven years later, find serious difficulties here. If Christians were really given grace in a separate rapture seven years before, they would not have expected till the end to receive it at the revelation of Christ. In the immediate context, Peter mentioned the Christian faith: ... *your faith (...) may be found to praise, honor, and glory at the revelation* (apokalupsis) *of Jesus Christ* (v. 7). Christians are waiting for the revelation (apokalupsis) of our Lord Jesus Christ (1 Corinthians 1:7). But once again, why would Christians be waiting for the "revelation" if the rapture were to happen seven years before?

According to the Bible, the *apokalupsis* –the revelation of Christ– will take place when the saints meet the Lord; this is the day they are waiting for. Then, the rapture cannot be an event and the revelation another one which occurs later. Instead of indicating two phases, the Greek words *parousia* and *apokalupsis* point to a single event: the second coming of Christ at the end of the world.

Another word used to describe the coming of the Lord, *epiphaneia,* refers to the manifestation and the glory with which our Lord will come back. Nobody applies this to a secret coming before the tribulation, because Christ will destroy the man of sin *with the brightness of His coming* (epiphaneia) *(2 Thessalonians 2:8).* If we consider this, we can see that believers must ... *keep this commandment without spot, blameless until our Lord Jesus Christ's appearing* (epiphaneia) *which He will manifest in His own time, He who is the blessed and only Potentate, the King of kings and Lord of lords (1 Timothy 6:14-15).* Why encouraging Christians to keep the commandment until the *epiphaneia* –the glorious appearing–, if the rapture were to occur seven years before it?

The fourth word on our list, *phaneroo,* means to reveal in reference to the open power and glory of the coming of Christ. *... when the Chief Shepherd appears* (phaneroo), *you will receive the crown of glory that does not fade away (1 Peter 5:4).* Which sense would these words make if Christians were raptured and crowned on an earlier coming? As John said: *... we know that when He is revealed, we shall be like Him, for we shall see Him as He is (1 John 3:2).*

As Christians, when Christ comes and appears, when he is revealed, we will be like Him.

There is no indication here of an invisible coming.

The Greek terms, instead of referring to two separate events, show quite the opposite. They are interchangeably used. Jesus said: *But as the days of Noah were, so also will the coming* (parousia) *of the Son of Man be (Matthew 24:37).* Luke describes the same passage this way: *... as it was in the days of Noah (...) Even so will it be in the day when the Son of Man is revealed* (apokalupsis) *(Luke 17:26-30). Therefore you also be ready, for the Son of Man is coming* (erchomai) *at an hour you do not expect (Matthew 24:44).* Here the words *parousia, apokalupsis* and *erchomai* are used to describe the same happening.

Erchomai is also used to describe the same happening as *heko*: *For yet a little while, and He who is coming* (erchomai) *will come* (heko) *and will not tarry (Hebrews 10:37).* The terms *heko* and *parousia* are used together: *Where is the promise of His coming* (parousia)? *(...) the day of the Lord will come* (heko) *as a thief in the night (2 Peter 3:4-10). Parousia* and *epiphaneia* are connected: *... the lawless one will be revealed, whom the Lord will (...) destroy with the brightness* (epiphaneai) *of his coming* (parousia) *(2 Thessalonians 2:8).* We know that the *parousia* is the *phaneroo* because two expressions are used together: *And now, little children, abide in Him, that when He appears* (phaneroo) *we may have confidence and not be ashamed before Him at His coming* (parousia) *(1 John 2:28).*

We see that all these Greek terms are used in an interchangeable way. Just like in English, different words have different nuances of the same meaning. Any attempt to divide the second coming into two stages, on the basis of an alleged distinction between the Greek terms, is totally artificial. When Jesus went up into heaven and his disciples stood gazing up, two angels told them: **Men of Galilee, why do you stand gazing up into heaven? This same Jesus, who was taken up from you into heaven, will so come in like manner as you saw Him go into heaven (Acts 1:11).** The fact that they "did not see" him go up into heaven on two moments is an argument which opposes his second coming in two stages.

11

THE RAPTURE OR CATCHING UP - PART 2

THE MILLENNIUM

*W*hen the Son of Man comes in His glory, and all the holy angels with Him, then He will sit on the throne of His glory.

—Matthew 25:31

For whoever is ashamed of Me and My words in this adulterous and sinful generation, of him the Son of Man also will be ashamed when He comes in the glory of His Father with the holy angels.
—Mark 8:38

THE COMING "FOR" AND "WITH" THE SAINTS

What can we say about the widespread idea that, just like Jesus will come "with" the saints (Jude 14), there must be an earlier coming of the Lord to take them up into heaven? In fact, the Bible never uses the expression "for" the saints. In the passage of the rapture, instead of saying that the believers will be raptured into heaven, it is said that they will be caught up in the clouds to meet the Lord in the air (1 Thessalonians 4:16-17). But the text does not explain where they go after meeting the Lord in the clouds.

When the Word declares that the saints will rise up to **meet** the Lord in the air, the word is *apantesis*. It is used to describe the visit of a king or a ruler to a city. While coming into town, he was welcomed by the citizens who travelled with him in the last part of his journey. If it means the same here, while Jesus Christ is descending from heaven, the believers will go up to "meet the Lord in the air" and come down with him. This does not refer to a separate coming. *Apantesis* appears again in the parable of the ten virgins who *took their lamps and went out to meet the bridegroom* (Matthew 25:1). After going out to "meet" him, they returned "with him".

There is another use of the term *apantesis* connected with Paul's journey to Rome: *And so we went toward Rome. And from there, when the brethren heard about us, they came to meet us as far as Apian Forum...* Let us suppose that the men who came to meet Paul talked about their plans; that they heard that Paul was coming to Rome and went out to meet him. The fact that it is not explained is not relevant. That going out would also include their coming back with him. Nobody would think that this meant that they would meet Paul, come back to the place where he had been and stay there for a while. Finally they would come to Rome with him.

I have been in the Christian ministry for more than twenty years, and I have travelled to the five continents, about sixty nations and hundreds of cities around the world. Almost with no exception, everywhere my hosts, pastors or leaders of the community, went to meet me at the airport to take me to their homes. They go out to meet me, "not" to come back with me to the place from which I have travelled, but to take me to the place which is arranged for me. In the Middle East, like in Latin America, they have the custom of meeting a guest at the gates or in the terminal of his arrival. This is literally what Paul writes will happen when Christ returns in his glory to reign in the midst of his Church.

Oswald J. Smith, a noted missionary statesman, pastor and author explains this in these words: "*I also learned that the word for "meet" in 1 Thessalonians 4 did not mean to 'remain at the meeting' point but to "return with". When the Roman brethren went out to meet Paul, they returned with him immediately. When the virgins met the bridegroom, they accompanied him back to the wedding. When the saints meet Christ in the air, they will return **with** him. There is no secret rapture. That theory must be deliberately read into the passage.*"[1]

Even if we do not consider the word "to meet" or the expression "comes with", Jude 14 cannot refer to the idea of two stages. There are good reasons to believe that the saints mentioned in this scripture are *angels* that will come with the Lord. *Behold, the Lord comes with ten thousands of His saints (Jude 14).* The term translated as "saints" is *hagios* which means simply "holy". It could be used with the meaning of angels as well as of men, but in this context we believe it refers to angels.

The *Pulpit Commentary* says: *It is preferable to say with ten thousands of his angels because the "holy ones" referred to here are*

1   Oswald Smith, Tribulation or Rapture-Which? (London: The Sovereign Grace Advent Testimony), p. 9.

angels.[2] This matches Jesus' words when he spoke of coming with the holy angels, having "holy" the same meaning as in Jude 14: *When the Son of Man comes in His glory and all the holy* (hagios) *angels with Him..." (Matthew 25:31). For whoever is ashamed of Me and My words in this adulterous and sinful generation, of him the Son of Man also will be ashamed when He comes in the glory of His Father with the holy* (hagios) *angels (Mark 8:38).*

The expression "ten thousands of his saints" (used in Jude 14) also appears in Deuteronomy 33:2. This is the general belief that this passage refers to the angels: *The LORD came from Sinai, and rose up from Seir unto them; He shined forth from Mount Paran, and He came with ten thousands of saints.* Again the Pulpit Commentary points out that it would be better to translate "with ten thousands of angels because it refers to them".[3] The Matthew Henry's Commentary makes the same point: ***His appearance was glorious He shone forth like the sun when He goes forth in His strength. Even Seir and Paran, two mountains at some distance, were illuminated by the divine glory which appeared on Mount Sinai... He came with his holy angels... Hence the law is said to be given by the disposition of angels (Acts 7:53, Hebrews 2:2).***[4]

If the expression "thousands of his saints" refers to angelic beings in Deuteronomy, it makes sense to believe that the same expression could mean angelic beings in Jude 14. The context holds this position because these saints are connected with Christ at the day of judgment against the wicked: *Behold, the Lord comes with ten thousands of His saints* (hagios) to execute judgment on all, to convict all who are ungodly *(Jude 14.15)*. We believe that this will be the work of angels, not of Christians. As the Bible says:

2   The Pulpit Commentary (Grand Rapids: Erdmann's Publishing Company, reprint 1950), Vol. 22, p. 12.

3   Ibid, Vol. 3, p.534.

4   Matthew Henry, Matthew Henry's Commentary (New York: Fleming H. Revell Company, reprint of 1721 edition), p. 874. Cf. Job 15:15; Psalms 89:5,7; Daniel 8:13; 4:13.

So it will be at the end of the age. The angels will come forth, separate the wicked from among the just, and cast them into the furnace of fire. Matthew 13:49-50

... when the Lord Jesus is revealed from heaven with His mighty angels, in flaming fire taking vengeance on those who do not know God... 2 Thessalonians 1:7

DOES IT HAVE A BIBLICAL FOUNDATION?

On one occasion the author read the whole New Testament with the purpose of identifying all the passages which teach that the coming of the Lord will be in two stages. I reached the same conclusion as Oswald J. Smith's: *We could go all through the writers of the New Testament and would not find a single indication of the alleged "two stages" of the coming of our Lord... There is no verse in the Bible that mentions them.*[5]

Men from different Christian denominations know and accept this position. The well-known Bible scholar G. Campbell Morgan says: *The idea of a separate and secret coming of Christ has... no biblical foundation whatsoever.*[6]

Pat Robertson made the following statement: *If we assume that the tribulation will be a time of persecution in the whole world, then I have to admit that Christians will go through it. I find no teaching in the Bible that Christians will be raptured before the tribulation. The Bible mentions two comings of Jesus. One is his*

---

5   Oswald Smith, op. cit., p. 10.
6   William R. Kimball, The Rapture, A Question of Timing (Grand Rapids: Baker Book House, 1985), p. 179, quoted from Christianity Today, August, 1959.

birth; the second one is his triumphal return. There is no third coming for a secret rapture.[7]

Even those who believe in rapture before the tribulation have accepted that there is not a single verse in the Bible that refers to this.

Wilfred Meloon once heard Charles Fuller say on his radio program: *There is no verse in the whole New Testament that teaches a rapture of the Church before the tribulation; but I still believe in it.* [8] He loved Charles Fuller, but he was flabbergasted at his words. How can a doctrine of any kind be of importance, when it has no biblical foundation?

Although the Bible does not mention two stages, those Christians who believe this theory think that it is justified by indirect evidence coming from certain "proof texts", which we will examine now. First of all, Revelation 4:1: ***After these things I looked, and behold, a door standing open in heaven. And the first voice which I heard was like a trumpet speaking with me, saying: "Come up here, and I will show you things which must take place after this".***

A CLEAR PICTURE OF THE RAPTURE?

Scofield says: *This call seems clearly to indicate the fulfillment of 1 Thessalonians 4:14-17 (the rapture). The word "church" does not appear again in the book of Revelation until all things have been fulfilled.*[9] De Haan repeats the same idea: *This passage in*

---

7   Pat Robertson Answers to 200 of Life's Most Probing Questions (Nashville: Thomas Nelson Publishers, 1984), pp. 155, 156.
8   Wilfred C. "Will" Meloon, Eschaton, Issue XVI (Orange City, FL: 1979).
9   Scofield, op. cit. p. 1334.

Revelation is one of the shortest ones, yet one of the clearest pictures in the Scriptures of the rapture of the Church.[10]

The word "church" does not appear in Revelation, in chapters 4 to 18; the dispensationalist theory is that the Church is not on earth during that time, and it is not mentioned again until chapter 19 which is about the marriage supper of the Lamb and the coming of Christ as King of kings. But if the absence of the word "church" can prove that the Church is not present in chapters 4 to 18, we should come to the conclusion that the Church is also absent in chapter 19, because this term is not mentioned in this chapter either! Nor is it in chapters 20 or 21. We only find these words in a final commentary in the last chapter: *I, Jesus, have sent My angel to testify to you these things in the churches.* It does not refer to the universal Church but to the seven churches in Asia (Revelation 22:16).

While the word "church "does not appear after chapter 3 until the last part of Revelation, this is not absent in those chapters. In Revelation 13:7 we read that the beast would *make war with the saints.* Verse 10 mentions *the patience and the faith of the saints.* (Their patience and faith in the middle of persecution) In chapter 16, verse 6 the "saints" are mentioned once again. In chapter 17 we read that the Babylon woman (the Roman Catholic Church) *was drunk with the blood of the saints* (v. 6) and that *in her was found the blood of prophets and saints* (Revelation 18:24).

The dispensationalist idea is that the saints mentioned in these chapters are not the Church believers, but those of the tribulation. Nevertheless, we find the word "saints" in chapter 19 where we are told that this refers to the Church. ... *the marriage of the Lamb has come, and His wife has made herself ready. And to*

---

10   M.R. De Haan, Thirty-five Simple Studies on the major Themes in Revelation (Grand Rapids: Zondervan, 1946).

*her it was granted to be arrayed in fine linen, clean and bright, for
the fine linen is the righteous acts of the saints* (Revelation 19:7-
8). The Scofield Bible commentary says: *The Lamb's wife is "the
bride", the Church.*[11] But for the sake of coherence, if the saints of
chapter 19 are the Church believers, how can we possibly discuss
the fact that the saints mentioned in the previous chapters (18,
17, 16 and 13) refer to something else? This makes no sense.

The rapture or catching up is not the subject in Revelation
4:1; it simply describes John's experience in the spirit: to be taken
up to the heavenly kingdom. This does not prove that we must
try to find the Church in heaven; being taken to Babylon would
not prove either that the Church was there (Revelation 17:3-
5). While the various scenes take place in Revelation, John is
found in different places; on the earth he sees an angel "coming
down from heaven" (Revelation 10:1, 18:1); he measures what
appears to be a temple on the earth, because "the holy city will be
trodden by the Gentiles" (Revelation 11:1-2); he stands and sees
a beast rising up out of the see (Revelation 13:1). It is evident
that John cannot be a symbol of the Church in heaven in those
chapters.

KEPT FROM THE HOUR OF TRIAL

Another passage in Revelation that proves the dispensationalist
theory has Jesus' words to the church in Philadelphia: *Because
you have kept My command to persevere, I also will keep you from
the hour of trial which shall come upon the whole world, to test those
who dwell on the earth (Revelation 3:10).* Those who use this verse
to defend the secret rapture doctrine believe that the "hour of
trial" is the same as the time of the "great tribulation" at the end

---

11   Scofield, op.cit. p.1348.

of this age. Then they have to admit that to be kept from this trial they have to be caught up from this world!

In its nearest application, this promise is for the church in Philadelphia, situated in Asia Minor during the first century. Were the believers of this church kept from a time of world trial? They were indeed, because the promise was sure. But for this, they did not have to be caught up. We believe God's power and grace kept them. If God was to keep his promise, the "hour of trial" –whatever exact meaning this expression may have– would have happened at that time. This is not proof at all of a secret rapture to escape from the period of the great tribulation, 2,000 years later.

Some believe that the seven churches in Asia represent the seven consecutive ages of the Church, which run from the first century to the rapture. If this is true, the message to the church in Philadelphia cannot refer to the rapture because Philadelphia was the sixth church in the succession, not the last one (the seventh one). If the message to the church in Philadelphia referred to an escaping rapture, the ages of the Church should be 1, 2, 3, 4, 5, 7 and 6!

Christians can be kept from an hour of trial, in any age, without being caught up from the world.

We can establish this principle by comparing the following passages:

Because you have kept My command to persevere, I also will keep you from the hour of trial which

shall come upon the whole world, to test those who dwell on the earth. Revelation 3:10

... they have kept Your word. I do not pray that You should take them out of the world, but that You should keep them from the evil one. John 17:6, 15

Both passages are Jesus' words. John is the author of the two of them. The people referred to in both passages have kept the Word. In one of them they are kept from the hour of trial; in the other one they are kept from evil. Like in the Lord's prayer, these expressions are closely related: *And do not lead us into temptation, but deliver us from the evil one (Matthew 6:13)*. If Christians can be kept from the evil of this world without being caught up, as we read in one of these passages, therefore they do not have to be raptured either to avoid being tempted.

Although Revelation 3:10 had probably a specific meaning and its fulfillment for the church in Philadelphia, there is also a promise of the power of God to deliver us from temptation any time, any century, any year, any day; not only in the last seven years of this present age. Paul wrote: *No temptation has overtaken you except such as is common to man; but God is faithful, who will not allow you to be tempted beyond what you are able, but with the temptation will also make the way of escape, that you may be able to bear it (1 Corinthians 10:13). ... the Lord knows how to deliver the godly out of temptations... (2 Peter 2:9)*. This was Jabez's prayer: *... that You would keep me from evil (...) So God granted him what he requested (1 Chronicles 4:10)*. And today, we can be kept *by the power of God through faith for salvation* (1 Peter 1:5). Because God *is able to keep you from stumbling* (Jude 24). God can provide us with his keeping power and the way to escape from temptation with no need for a secret rapture.

WHAT SHALL WE ESCAPE FROM?

Let us see one more scripture: *Watch therefore, and pray always that you may be counted worthy to escape all these things that will come to pass, and to stand before the Son of Man (Luke 21:36).* This refers to pray to be able to "escape" but, again, there is no mention to the Church rapture from this world with this aim. Jesus prayed: *I do not pray that You should take them out of the world, but that You should keep them from the evil one (John 17:15).* Would Jesus pray in a certain way and later would tell his disciples to act in a different way?

What is the word "escape" linked with? Is it an escape during a period of time, of the dispensationalist great tribulation in the last seven years of this age? It does not make reference to this. If we consider the context, we realize it mentions "that day" when Christians will be caught up to meet the Lord in the air, and then destruction will fall upon the earth.

> *Heaven and earth will pass away (...) But take heed to yourselves, lest your hearts be weighed down with carousing, drunkenness, and cares of this life, and that Day come on you unexpectedly. For it will come as a snare on all those who dwell on the face of the whole earth. Watch therefore, and pray always that you may be counted worthy to escape all these things that will come to pass, and to stand before the Son of Man. Luke 21:33-36*

If believers were not on the earth because they have been caught up seven years before the end, how could that day suddenly come upon them?

Jesus promised that those who watch in prayer and are not filled with gluttony and drunkenness will escape from the destruction on "that day". Paul wrote the same basic message:

> *For you yourselves know perfectly that the day of the Lord so comes as a thief in the night. For when they say: "Peace and safety!" then sudden destruction comes upon them, as labor pains upon a pregnant woman. And they shall not escape. But you, brethren, are not in darkness, so that this Day should overtake you as a thief. You are all sons of light and sons of the day. We are not of the night nor of darkness. Therefore let us not sleep, as others do, but let us watch and be sober (...) For God did not appoint us to wrath, but to obtain salvation through our Lord Jesus Christ. 1 Thessalonians 5:2-9*

Let us notice that this passage also mentions "that day" which will bring "sudden destruction" upon the wicked and they will not escape. On the contrary, Christians will be able to escape. God has not appointed them to wrath. They will be caught up to meet the Lord in heaven while destruction falls upon the earth.

WILL CHRIST COME BACK "AT ANY TIME"?

Did the early Christians believe that the rapture could happen at *any* time? Or did they believe that certain things had to come to pass *first*?

We believe that in the New Testament there are convincing proofs that the early Church did not believe in this idea of "at any time."

Jesus declared that no man knew the time of his coming and that we must always be watchful and obedient.

However, Jesus himself taught that certain things had to come to pass first.

When Jesus spoke to the disciples about his second coming, he was still with them. It is obvious that he had to ascend into heaven, before coming to the earth for the second time. Before his ascension, of course, he would go to Calvary: ***But first He must suffer many things and be rejected by this generation (Luke 17:25).***

Jesus told his disciples that after ascending into heaven, he would send the Holy Spirit. Obviously, this would happen before he came again. Before Pentecost, we see the disciples waiting for, not the second coming of Christ, but the coming of the Holy Spirit to fill them with power. Empowered with the Holy Spirit, they would go to every nation and to the end of the earth to teach people (Acts 1:8). They needed time to travel, preach, baptize and train the newly converted Christians. In all probability, Jesus would not return before they were able to carry out what He had commanded them to do!

Jesus predicted the destruction of Jerusalem and warned his disciples:

> *But when you see Jerusalem surrounded by armies, then know that its desolation is near. Then let those who are in Judea flee to the mountains, let those who are in the midst of her depart, and let not those who are in the country enter her. Luke 21:20-21*

On the second coming of Christ, believers will not have to flee to the mountains because they will be caught up to meet the Lord in the air. Therefore, the destruction of Jerusalem would be an event *before* the second coming of Christ. Living this side of the fulfillment, we do know that Jerusalem was destroyed in the year 70 A.D.

Jesus also explained that Peter was going to grow old and die "before" his second coming! ... *when you are old, you will stretch out your hands, and another will gird you and carry you where you do not wish. This He spoke, signifying by what death he would glorify God* (John 21:18-19; see 2 Peter 1:14). Then Peter asked the Lord if John was going to live to see his coming; Jesus replied: *If I will that he remain till I come, what is that to you? You follow Me. Then this saying went out among the brethren that this disciple would not die. Yet Jesus did not say to him that he would not die, but, If I will that he remain till I come, what is that to you?* (John 21:20-23). He did not say if John was going to live until his second coming, but he told Peter that he would grow old and die before his return.

The early Christians lived with the expectation and hope of the second coming, because if they were alive at that moment or were raised, at the end they would take part in the glory of that day. But they did not believe that his coming would occur at any time; they knew that certain things would come to pass first.

When Paul wrote to the Thessalonians, he mentioned the resurrection and the catching up of Christians to meet the Lord in the air (1 Thessalonians 4:16-17). Later on, they were confused about this glorious event; for that reason, in his second letter, Paul made the matter clear. His words show that he did not believe in the idea of "at any time":

> *Now, brethren, concerning the coming of our Lord Jesus Christ and our gathering together to Him, we ask you, not to be soon shaken in mind or troubled, either by spirit or by word or by letter, as if from us, as though the day of Christ had come. Let no one deceive you by any means; for that Day will not come unless (#1) the falling away comes first, and (#2) the man of sin is revealed, the son of perdition. 2 Thessalonians 2:1-3*

Two things are mentioned here that Christians will see *before* the coming of Christ to catch up his saints. There will be a falling away and the man of sin will be revealed. Regarding these things the apostle, under the inspiration of the Holy Spirit, said: *"Let no one deceive you"*. We should be careful with the teaching that the Church will be raptured *before* the man of sin is revealed. According to Paul, the order of these events will be: (1) the falling away; (2) the revelation of the man of sin; (3) the coming of Christ and our meeting with him. This is clear. But according to the dispensationalist point of view: at any time, instead of following this sequence, the events will take place this way: (3) then (1) and lastly (2). This is: (3) the coming of Christ and our meeting with him; (1) the falling away; (2) the revelation of the man of sin; 3, 1, 2 or maybe 3, 2, 1, instead of 1, 2, and 3.

In an attempt to justify this inverted order, some teach that the apostasy is the disappearance of the Church during the catching up. But the term translated as "falling away" is the Greek word *apostasia* which means a deviation of the truth, a well-established meaning. The attempt to change "apostasy" for "rapture" shows how difficult the dispensationalist theory is.

Paul said that believers would see certain events first: the falling away, the revelation of the man of sin and then, the catching up to meet the Lord in his coming. If the apostasy were a rapture, an exodus of Christians from the world, they would not see the things that will happen next because they would not be here. Paul's words would not have any connection with his declaration.

Being afflicted by persecutions and tribulations, the believers in Thessalonica wondered if the day of the Lord was near (2 Thessalonians 2:1). If Paul had believed in the "at any time" position, here he would have the perfect opportunity to encourage them with the teaching that Jesus was coming back soon, at any time. He could have written something like this: "Now, brethren, concerning the coming of our Lord Jesus Christ and our gathering together to Him, we ask you, not to be soon shaken in mind or troubled, *because nothing should come first*. For that Day will come *before* the falling away and *before* the man of sin is revealed. Yes, our gathering together to Him can happen *at any time*".

On the contrary, those were not his words. He explained that there would be an apostasy and that the man of sin would be revealed before the day of Christ. He cannot have been wrong; the day of Christ refers to the catching up because it is used regarding our *gathering together to Him* (2 Thessalonians 2). Christians are waiting for *the day of our Lord Jesus Christ* (1

Corinthians 1:7-9). Christians will be caught up in *the day of the Lord Jesus*, and they will be each other's boast (2 Corinthians 1:14). The good work that the Lord has begun in his children must continue *until the day of Jesus Christ* (Philippians 1:6). Paul encourages the Philippian believers to be blameless and harmless for *the day of Christ* (v 10), when he sees them and may rejoice that he has not labored in vain (Philippians 2:15-16). All these scriptures clearly show that the "day of Christ" is the moment when Christians will meet him.

Scofield, trying to face the evident problem here for dispensationalists, says that the King James Version did a wrong translation of "the day of Christ" (2 Thessalonians 2:2); and it should have been "the day of the Lord".[12] Apparently, in some ancient manuscripts we read one thing and in others, we read something different. Which is the difference? We use the expression "the coming of the Lord" when we refer to "the coming of Christ". Why should we give a different meaning to the expressions in the New Testament "the day of the Lord and "the day of Christ"? Only an attempt to defend a wrong theory would make this distinction. The following terms are interchangeably used with regard to the coming of the Lord to meet his saints:

- "The day of Christ" (Philippians 1:10)

- "The day of Jesus Christ" (Philippians 1:6)

- "The day of our Lord Jesus Christ" (1 Corinthians 1:8)

- "The day of the Lord Jesus" (2 Corinthians 1:14)

- "The day of the Lord" (1 Thessalonians 5:2)

---

12   Ibid, p. 1212

We think it is inconsistent to try and change the sense of the last expression to give a different meaning to "Lord", or a different time from the one described in the other terms. The day of the Lord is the same day than the day of Christ in the New Testament. According to Paul, that day, when Christians will be caught up, will not come until the man of sin has been revealed.

WHEN DID ALL THIS BEGIN?

The teaching of a secret coming, before the revelation of the man of sin, has been widely spread and is currently believed in this present century. Many Christians have accepted it without further investigation or questioning of any kind. It may be shocking for some, but this doctrine was not the position of the early Church or the reformers until around 1830. If this is true, the teaching of a secret rapture before the tribulation is not a part of the true original faith given to believers. It is not the original gospel.

George Ladd, Bible institute teacher, after presenting a view of the Church history, said: *All the fathers of the Church who have written about this matter think that the Church will suffer at the hands of the Antichrist… we can find no trace of pre-tribulationalism in the early Church; and modern pre-tribulationists have not proven that this theory was the belief of some of the fathers of the Church or the Word scholars before the XIX century.*[13]

This declaration can be dramatic, but we believe that it will prevail after looking into it. The *didache*, one of the first works of Christian literature written after the New Testament, declares that the antichrist would come, that many would be offended and lost and that the resurrection of the righteous would follow

---

13   George E. Ladd, The Blessed Hope (Grand Rapids: Erdmann's, 1956), p.31.

(not before but after) this time of sadness.[14] Barnabas' letter, written around the same time, says: *When the Son appears, He will destroy the reign of the evil one (in reference to Satan and not the antichrist) and will judge the wicked;* this way he puts the coming of Christ after the reign of the evil one and not before it. He did not believe in a coming of Christ at any time because he expected the fall of the Roman Empire first.[15]

Justin Martyr (100-165) referred to the coming of Christ in these words: *He will descend from heaven in glory, when the man of apostasy speaking strange things against the Most High will try to do illegal acts on the earth against Christians who have learnt the true worship to God, the law and the Word which came out from Jerusalem through Jesus' apostles. Christ will come from heaven in glory with his angels, when he will raise the bodies of all men who ever lived and will clothe the worthy's in immortality.*[16]

Irenaeus (130-202) spoke about the resurrection of the righteous, which takes place *after* the coming of the Antichrist. *But when the Antichrist has devastated all things on earth... then the Lord will come from heaven in the clouds, in the glory of the father, sending this man and his followers to the lake of fire; but bringing the righteous into the times of the Kingdom.* He mentioned the kings who will give their kingdoms to the beast and will make *the Church* flee. *After this, they will be destroyed by the coming of the Lord... At the end the Church will be raptured and, having overcome, will be crowned incorruptible.*[17]

Tertullian (160-240) believed that the Antichrist would rise to power and would persecute *the Church.* He said that as a habit

---

14   Ibid.
15   Barnabas, in Ante-Nicene Fathers, Vol. 1, pp.146, 138.
16   Justin, Dialogue with Trypho, chapter 52.
17   Irenaeus, Against Heresies, 35:1, 30:4, 26:1, 29:1.

Christians should pray to take part in the resurrection and meet Christ at the end of this age.[18]

Hippolytus (170-236) spoke about the four empires in Daniel and said that with the fall of the fourth empire (which was in power), the terrible Antichrist would appear and persecute the Church. He believed that the second coming would be the time when the dead would be risen, the Antichrist destroyed and the saints glorified.[19]

Cyprian (200-258), Christian bishop and martyr, believed that the Antichrist would reign over the world and that after his reign, Christ would come at the end of the world.[20]

Lactantius (260-330) believed that the Antichrist would reign over the world and afflict the righteous, but that God would send a great king to rescue them, destroy the wicked with fire and the sword, raise the dead and renew the earth.[21]

Cyril (315-386), bishop of Jerusalem, wrote: "*We believe in Him, who ascended also to heaven, and was seated to the right hand of the Father, and will come in glory to judge the living and the dead... at the end of this world, in the last day. For of this world there is to be an end, and this created world is to be remade anew*".[22] It is evident, due to several statements, that he believed that the Antichrist would rise to power and persecute the Church before the second coming of Christ.

The essence of the teaching of these ancient writers is that the Antichrist would persecute the Church; the coming of Christ would follow bringing an end to the reign of the Antichrist; and

---

18   Tertullian, On the Resurrection of the Flesh, chapter twenty-two.
19   Hippolytus, Treatise on Christ and Antichrist, chapters 66, 67.
20   Cyprian, Epistle 55.
21   Lactantius, the Divine Institutes, Vol.7.
22   The Catechetical Lectures of St Cyril, Lecture 15.

the end of the world would be the time of the resurrection when the saints will be gathered to meet the Lord.

Those who support the idea of the pre-tribulation usually quote Irenaeus: *And for that reason it is said that when the Church is suddenly caught up, there will be great tribulation such as has not been since the beginning of the world until this time, nor ever will be. This is the last battle of the righteous in which they will overcome and will be crowned with incorruption.*[23] Indeed, one part of this passage seems to teach a pre- tribulation rapture, but if we read the entire passage we realize it is not the intended meaning.

Iranaeus mentioned the tribulation as the "last" battle of the righteous that would overcome and be crowned; he also referred to the end as the time when the Church would be suddenly caught up. We have mentioned earlier that he believed the Antichrist would persecute the Church and after that, Christ would return to reward the righteous and destroy the wicked. Certainly this is not the dispensationalist pre-tribulation theory.

Over the centuries, there are certain outstanding names in the Christian history: John Wycliffe, John Huss, Martin Luther, Philipp Melanchthon, Huldreich Zwingli, William Tyndale, Nicholas Ridley, Hugh Latimer, John Foxe, Edwin Sandys, John Calvin, John Knox, King James, Isaac Newton, Thomas Newton, and John Wesley. NONE of these men believed that the Church would be caught up before the Antichrist was revealed. They all believed and taught that the Church would suffer at his hands and that the coming of Christ would put an end to his reign.

Out of consideration for those who still believe in the doctrine of a secret rapture, among whom there are some dear friends and ministers, it is our sincere conviction that this must be rejected.

---

23   Irenaeus, op.cit. 5:29.

First, because it lacks solid scriptural support; and secondly, because its origin is relatively new. Although the idea of a secret rapture is still greatly publicized, many within the body of Christ are beginning to analyze the issue of the rapture.

WHAT ABOUT THE MILLENNIUM?

The rise of Dispensationalism and Escapism in the Protestant Evangelical Churches coincided with the rise of Pietism and Armenianism. If Christians do not believe that the moral law of God is tied to the nations, that God has already predetermined who will and who will not be saved, then they are not challenged to change their lives or anyone else's. If they believe the world belongs to Satan, they will have a pessimistic view of the future, indeed a fatalistic view. These people will embrace the eschatological view that relieves them of any moral or social responsibilities and the stewardship of God's creation. Their idea is that at Christ's second coming will take care of all evils. They point to a 1000 year theocratic reign of Christ when all things will be well when Satan is bound during that period.

Dispensational premillennialists hold that Christ will come before a seven-year period of intense tribulation to take His church (living and dead) into heaven. After this period of fulfillment of divine wrath, He shall then return to rule from a holy city (i.e., the New Jerusalem) over the earthly nations for one thousand years. After these thousand years, Satan, who was bound up during Christ's earthly reign, will be loosed to deceive the nations, gather an army of the deceived, and take up to battle against the Lord. This battle will end in both the judgment of the wicked and Satan and the entrance into the eternal state of glory by the righteous.[24]

---

24   www.blueletterbible.org

The interpretation of Rev. 20 is related to a hermeneutical interpretation of the ten much debated verses. An analytical study of the millennium must be best understood in the light of the numerical usage of the Bible. Biblical usage of numbers is common, for example the number 7 or the number 12 or the number 3 or the number 40 all these have a significance in Bible interpretation; so does the number 10 which represents total completion. These are used to imply extensions like 12 x 12 = 144 and extended will represent 12,000 x 12,000 = 144,000. You can see the usage in Revelation 5.11, 7.4-8, 9.16, 11.3, 12.6, 14.1,3 and 20.

In Psalms 50.10 it states that the Lord owns the cattle on a **thousand hills.** Does this mean that all cattle in the remaining hills are owned by someone else? The implied content is that He owns ALL the cattle. **Thousands** refers to an undefined and vast number. You can see it's usage in Deut. 1.11, 7.9, Ps. 68.17, 84.10, 90.4. There are many other examples of biblical numerical use that represent multiplied numbers. The millennium is NOT a literal number of years but represents the reign of Christ through the Church as he rules the Earth through the life changing power of the Gospel as we reign with him as kings and priests and as He reigns as King of kings and Lord of lords.

There is a definite return to the original, historical and apostolic position.

This has been one of the most important concepts of the apostolic and prophetic movement in the new apostolic reformation.

CHAPTER

12

THE ONE HUNDRED AND FORTY-FOUR THOUSAND

PAST OR FUTURE?

And I heard the number of those who were sealed. One hundred and forty-four thousand of all the tribes of the children of Israel were sealed: of the tribe of Judah twelve thousand were sealed; of the tribe of Reuben twelve thousand were sealed; of the tribe of Gad twelve thousand were sealed; of the tribe of Asher twelve thousand were sealed; of the tribe of Naphtali twelve thousand were sealed; of the tribe of Manasseh twelve thousand were sealed; of the tribe of Simeon *twelve thousand were sealed; of the tribe of Levi twelve thousand were sealed; of the tribe of Issachar twelve thousand were sealed; of the tribe of Zebulon twelve thousand were sealed; of the tribe of Joseph twelve thousand were sealed; of the tribe of Benjamin twelve thousand were sealed.*

–Revelation 7:4-8

Then I looked, and behold, a Lamb standing on Mount Zion, and with Him one hundred and forty-four thousand, having His Father's name written on their foreheads. And I heard a voice from heaven, like the voice of many waters, and like the voice of loud thunder. And I heard the sound of harpists playing their harps. They sang as it were a new song before the throne, before the four living creatures, and the elders; and no one could learn that song except the hundred and forty-four thousand who were redeemed from the earth.[4] These are the ones who were not defiled with women, for they are virgins. These are the ones who follow the Lamb wherever He goes. These were redeemed from among men, being first fruits to God and to the Lamb. And in their mouth was found no deceit, for they are without fault before the throne of God. –Revelation 14: 1-5

THE FIRST OR THE LAST FRUIT?

Nowadays, most Christians think that the 144,000 will appear in the future.

The most popular version of this idea is probably the futurist or dispensationalist one. The futurist theory says that the appearance of the 144,000 sealed will be during the last seven years (or three years and a half, according to some). They will be the "Jewish Pauls" who will preach the gospel of the Kingdom all around the world "after the disappearance of the Church."

In my opinion, this theory contradicts the Word of God. The book of Revelation presents many symbolisms of which we should pay attention to two main points:

1. The 144,000 will come from *all the tribes of the children of Israel (Rev. 7:4).*

2. The 144,000 will be redeemed *from among men, being first fruits to God and to the Lamb (Rev. 14:4).*

The first item refers to their identity. They are "Israelites". Although in the New Testament, the word "Israel" is sometimes used in a way that includes all believers, regardless of their race or nationality (Galatians 3:29; 6:16). But the verses about Israel, in contrast to the Gentiles, present a clear distinction in its use (Romans 1:16; 2:9; Acts 13:45-46). It is possible to see this contrast in the passage of the 144,000.

The 144,000 belong to *all the tribes of the children of Israel.* Then, in verse 9 we read: *After these things I looked, and behold, a great multitude which no one could number, of all nations, tribes, peoples, and tongues, standing before the throne and before the Lamb* (emphasis added by the author). Here we have a big group of Gentiles redeemed by the Lamb. In this multitude which no one could number, we find the 144,000 of "Israel" and people of all nations.

We agree with the idea that they are 144,000 Israelites, but not with the fact that these are redeemed as "first fruits" to God and to the Lamb.

In the Old Testament the word *first fruits* refers to the "first" results of the harvest that was presented to the Lord as an offering (Exodus 23:19, Leviticus 2:14, Nehemiah 10:35). In the New Testament, Christ is *the first to rise from the dead (Acts 26:23),* that is why he is mentioned as *the first fruits of those who have fallen asleep (1 Corinthians 15:20).* In 1 Corinthians 16:15 we read about the first converted Christians in Achaia this way: ... *you know the household of Stephanas, which it is the first fruits of Achaia*; likewise here, the first fruits to the Lamb are the "first converted Israelites".

There is no way the 144,000 could be *the first fruits* if they are not going to appear until the end times; in that case, they would be the last fruits.

THE 144,000... JEWS?

If we read the Word with careful attention, we realize that the first converted Christians were Jewish. In the first place, Jesus was sent to the "lost sheep" of the nation of Israel. On the day of Pentecost, the first disciples filled with the Holy Spirit were a group of Israelites; then 3,000 Jews were the first fruits of the Church, men of all the tribes of Israel who were in that city (Acts 2:5,22,29,36; 3:26). The gospel was first preached in Jerusalem (Acts 1:8, Luke 24:47).

The Bible tells us that thousands of Israelites accepted the Lord: *And when they heard it, they glorified the Lord. And they said to him: You see, brother, how many myriads of Jews there are who have believed, and they are all zealous for the law (Acts 21:20).* Paul wrote about Jews of the twelve tribes: *To this promise our twelve tribes, earnestly serving God night and day, hope to attain (Acts 26:7).*

James refers to those of the twelve tribes who have become Christians in these words: *James, a bondservant of God and of the Lord Jesus Christ, to the twelve tribes which are scattered abroad: Greetings (James 1:1).* The apostle calls them "first fruits" of His creatures (1:18), a perfect reference to the 144,000 Jews of the twelve tribes of Israel. They were possibly 144,000 in number. Nevertheless, this seems to be a symbolic number and for that reason there is no need for a mathematically exact number.

The 144,000 *are the ones who were not defiled with women, for they are virgins* (Rev. 14:4). That this scripture refers only to virgin single men would not be a correct interpretation. Every believer is married to Christ being spiritually virgin; there is no more difference between male and female; for that reason we can present ourselves faultless in the presence of his glory (Jude 24). We are a glorious Church, not having spot or wrinkle (Ephesians 5:27).

According to the futurist interpretation, the 144,000 will be converted at the *end* times; while the book of Revelation declares that they will be the *first fruits to the Lamb.* Millions of people have accepted Christ as their personal Savior in the last 2,000 years; how could a group of people in the future then be the first fruits?

Some futurists believe that the Church will not preach the gospel to every nation. Nowadays, we know that people all around the world have been reached for Christ. Others think that only these 144,000, without the presence of the Holy Spirit, will be able to carry out in a few years what the Church has not done in 2,000 years with the presence and power of the Holy Spirit. Undoubtedly, these **preachers** will perform a wonderful task; but, which part of the Bible says that the 144,000 will be preachers?

God has not finished his work with
the Jewish people yet.

Paul declares that **if the first fruit is holy, the lump is also holy (Romans 11:16).** Later on, he says that the Jews have become blind in part but in the end, "all Israel" will be saved: ... **that blindness in part has happened to Israel until the fullness of the Gentiles has come in. And so all Israel will be saved (Romans 11:25).** According to the Bible, all Israel will be saved, they will not save everyone.

In this chapter we have presented the explanation which, in our opinion, is most correct about the 144,000. I do not agree with the opinion held by Jehovah's witnesses or dispensationalists; however, we are referring to the symbolism of the book of Revelation and its interpretation can lead to different conclusions. We must stand firm in our own position based on the truth of the Word of God, just as we understand it, without being an instrument of division or argument *endeavoring to keep the unity of the Spirit in the bond of peace (...) speaking the truth in love (Ephesians 4:3,15).*

13

REDISCOVERING THE PRINCIPLES OF THE KINGDOM

*A*nd this gospel of the kingdom will be preached in the whole world as a testimony to all nations, and then the end will come.

—Matthew 24:14, NIV

This good news of the kingdom will be proclaimed to men all over the world as a witness to all the nations, and the end will come.–Matthew 24:14, J.B. Phillips New Testament

THE GOOD NEWS OF THE KINGDOM

The message of the Bible is not "religion", which is a human idea. Its main message in the whole New Testament is about the good news of the Kingdom.

Its main subjects include a kingdom, a king, a royal family and the colonization of the King's property; the re conquest of the Kingdom of this world; the creation of its government and empire through God's conquest and dominion over his creation. Therefore, we need to rediscover all truth in it which is hidden or has been misinterpreted. This is the reason why God is raising apostolic and prophetic ministries in his Church.

The words *kingdom* or *kingdoms* is used 156 times in the New Testament. In Matthew they appear fifty-five times; thirty-six of them refer to the "Kingdom of Heaven" and the rest to the "Kingdom of God". In Mark they appear twenty times; in Luke, forty-six times; in John, five times; and in Acts eight times. Paul uses them sixteen times. John the Baptist preached the message of the coming of the Kingdom of Heaven (Matthew 3:2). At the beginning of his ministry, Jesus used the term as the reason why he had been sent by the Father.

> *But he said: "I must proclaim the good news of the kingdom of God to the other towns also, because that is why I was sent". Luke 4:43, NIV*

> *He left the next day for open country. But the crowds went looking and, when they found him, clung to him so he couldn't go on. He told them: "Don't you realize that there are yet other villages where I have to tell the Message of God's kingdom, that this is the work God sent me to do?" Meanwhile he continued preaching in the meeting places of Galilee. Luke 4:42-44, The Message*

As we have already mentioned before, doctrines, traditions and paradigms we have inherited from religion, society or culture which resemble a distorted mirror stop us from seeing the light or receiving revelation; also the voices of those people who have had a profound impact on our minds through their work, actions and teachings.

The Holy Spirit is the one who brings the revelation that helps us understand the purpose and principles of the Kingdom.

Today, the Church preaches the gospel of Jesus Christ or of salvation, not the gospel preached by the Lord. Jesus never preached about himself; He spoke about the Kingdom and this is the message He sent his disciples to preach. Of course, we have to share the message of salvation, but mainly we have received the command to preach and teach the gospel of the Kingdom. *But go rather to the lost sheep of the house of Israel. And as you go, preach, saying: 'The kingdom of heaven is at hand' (Matthew 10:6-7).*

After his death and resurrection, Jesus presented himself to his disciples and spent 40 days with them, teaching and speaking to them about the Kingdom of God: *After his suffering, he presented himself to them and gave many convincing proofs that he was alive. He appeared to them over a period of forty days and spoke about the kingdom of God (Acts 1:3, NIV).*

The book of Acts tells us that the disciples taught about:

1) The Kingdom of God, and

2) Jesus Christ.

Paul's preaching and teaching was also about the Kingdom and the King.

But when they believed Philip as he proclaimed the good news of the kingdom of God and the name of Jesus Christ, they were baptized, both men and women. Acts 8:12, NIV

So when they had appointed him a day, many came to him at his lodging, to whom he explained and solemnly testified of the kingdom of God, persuading them concerning Jesus from both the Law of Moses and the Prophets, from morning till evening. Acts 28:23 **(emphasis added by the author)**

Then Paul dwelt two whole years in his own rented house, and received all who came to him, preaching the kingdom of God and teaching the things which concern the Lord Jesus Christ with all confidence, no one forbidding him.. Acts 28:30-31 **(emphasis added by the author)**

In Ephesus, Paul preached about the Kingdom of God for three months. This was a city filled with idolatry where all the religions of the world converged; for that reason, the philosophical fortresses that were in need of the message of the Kingdom to be broken, show the power of God. In his letter to the Romans, Paul declares that the Kingdom of God is not eating or drinking, but righteousness, peace and joy in the Holy Spirit. The word *peace* which matches the Hebrew term *shalom*, is usually translated into Greek as *soteria* or *soterion* and means:

Fullness, entirety, integrity, health, well-being, safety, solidity, tranquility, prosperity, perfection, rest, harmony. The absence of discord or agitation. Shalom comes from the verb root shalam, which means: "perfect, full or complete". Therefore, shalom represents a lot more than the absence of war or conflict; it is the fullness that all humanity tries to find.[1]

> *For the kingdom of God is not a matter of talk but of power. 1 Corinthians 4:20, NIV*

> *And my speech and my preaching were not with persuasive words of human wisdom, but in demonstration of the Spirit and of power, that your faith should not be in the wisdom of men but in the power of God. 1 Corinthians. 2:4-5*

The kingdom of God is the government of God in action. The Church has done a fairly decent job of preaching the gospel of Salvation, the significance of the Cross, the message of faith, but I am not sure knows what is the Gospel of the Kingdom.

Jesus declared: *I am the door (John 10:9), I am the way (John 14:6).* He did not say that He was the destination; the door is the access to a building, the way is the route or road to the final destination. He guides us and lets us come into his Kingdom. Nowadays, we bring people to the door but we leave them there; we show them the way but do not go with them on their journey; we lead them to salvation but abandon them at the beginning of their new life.

> *... He rescued us from the power of darkness, and re-established us in the kingdom of his beloved Son. Colossians1:13, J.B. Phillips New Testament*

> *... He has rescued us from the dominion of darkness and brought us into the kingdom of the Son he loves. Colossians 1:13, NIV*

---

1   Hayford, Jack W., General Editor, Plenitud Bible, (Nashville, TN: Editorial Caribe) 2000, c1994.

The new birth rescues us from the powers and the authority of the kingdom of darkness; we pass from being under the authority of Satan to being under the authority and the Kingdom of Christ.

We are rescued from a terrorist government to enjoy the freedom of a righteous nation. We have a new heavenly citizenship and, together with it, we enjoy the rights which are the benefits of that kingdom. It is a matter of immigration, of legal citizenship.

We pass to being under a new dominion. The word *dominion* means: sovereign or supreme authority, a ruled territory which is a synonym of control, rule, state, authority and jurisdiction. This has to do not only with the Kingdom, but also with its power and glory. He is the supreme king, the supreme power and the supreme glory.

In the prayer we read in Matthew 6: 9-13, Jesus taught us which our priorities should be when we pray: *Your kingdom come. Your will be done on earth as it is in heaven*; then He declares in verse 13: *For Yours is the kingdom and the power and the glory forever. Amen.*

DEFINITION OF KINGDOM

A kingdom is the sovereign reign and the ruling influence of a king or a ruler over his territory; that area on which he has dominion and makes an impact through his will, his intention and his purposes. It is a community of citizens who, through their lives and actions, express a culture that reflects the king's character and lifestyle. It is a nation ruled by a king who is guided by the will of the ruler.

When Jesus declared: "Repent, for the Kingdom of heaven is here or at hand", what he was saying in today's language is: "You must change your way of thinking and the path or way you are following".

A kingdom is made of the following items:

1. A king
2. A lord
3. A territory
4. A constitution
5. A number of laws and decrees
6. Keys and principles
7. Citizens
8. Royal privileges
9. A code of ethics
10. A community culture
11. A tax system
12. An army
13. A delegated authority
14. Ambassadors
15. An education system
16. Provision systems
17. Networks of influence
18. Grace and favor
19. A reputation or testimony
20. A principle of giving

Every government has certain requirements for its citizens. One of them is the payment of taxes on the income of people. If someone does not pay his taxes, he loses his privileges. If someone breaks a law, he loses his freedom or his citizen privileges. But if a person is a citizen who was born within the borders of the nation, he cannot lose his citizenship in "any" way, unless he renounces it of his own free will.

Taxes are the equivalent of tithes, what we pay for the government to work properly; offerings are a symbol of charity and good will.

Our mission: to colonize the Earth

God's plan from the beginning was to create the Earth and let his most precious handwork man colonize it.

He wanted man to rule and reign over his creation. For that reason He delegated the authority to rule and have dominion to him. His desire was to bring heaven and the principles of the Kingdom down to earth (Psalm 8:5-6):

> *God spoke: "Let us make human beings in our image, make them reflecting our nature so they can be responsible for the fish in the sea, the birds in the air, the cattle, and, yes, Earth itself, and every animal that moves on the face of Earth". God created human beings; he created them godlike, reflecting God's nature. He created them male and female. God blessed them: "Prosper! Reproduce! Fill Earth! Take charge! Be responsible for fish in the sea and*

birds in the air, for every living thing that moves on the face of Earth". Genesis 1:26-28, The Message

Here the Lord entrusts man with the task of colonizing the Earth with heaven to fill it with a heavenly culture. God did not create the planet earth as a temporary house for his creation; but as a permanent and eternal place where human beings could enjoy his communion and fellowship.

> *For this is what the Lord says—he, who created the heavens, he is God; he who fashioned and made the earth, he founded it; he did not create it to be empty, but formed it to be inhabited—he says: "I am the Lord, and there is no other". Isaiah 45:18, NIV*

Why would God want to remove us from the place He created for us to inhabit? Or why would we want to leave the place specially prepared for us by God?

> *May you be blessed by the LORD, who made heaven and earth. The heaven, even <u>the heavens, are the Lord's</u>; but <u>the earth He has given to the children of men.</u> Psalm 115:15-16* (emphasis added by the author)

TAKING POSSESSION OF THE EARTH

We have the calling from God to be kings and priests for Him; kings over his creation and priests of his Church.

The Lord is callings us to rule and reign to have dominion and, in that way, to establish his lordship to re conquer the kingdoms of this world and put his enemies under his feet. We are here to reign until Jesus returns. The *DOMINION* that the Church is called to establish has to be through it's positive input and influence in the culture and society of the nations.

We must live and love as citizens of this Kingdom (Philippians 3:20). Our mission is to be ambassadors, or authorized representatives holding the power of his Kingdom (2 Corinthians. 5:20). In order to be able to carry out this task, we need to use the resources of the Kingdom. We are soldiers who serve in his royal army and we are called to possess the Earth, the place where we live that has been given to us by Him to be maintained, planted and owned.

After his death, Christ ascended into heaven for a brief period to account for his finished work before the Ancient of Days (The Father). Daniel chapter 7 is an account of what happened between the time of his death and his return to earth to be with his disciples for forty days; during that period, He gave them power and authority (Matthew 28:18) and explained to them all about the Kingdom they had just received.

> *In my vision at night I looked, and there before me was one like a son of man, coming with the clouds of heaven. He approached the Ancient of Days and was led into his presence. He was given authority, glory and sovereign power; all nations and peoples of every language worshiped him. His dominion is an everlasting dominion that will not pass away, and his kingdom is one that will never be destroyed. Daniel 7:13-14, NIV*

> *But the holy people of the Most High will receive the kingdom and will possess it forever—yes, forever and ever. Daniel 7:18, NIV*

Then the sovereignty, power and greatness of all the kingdoms under heaven will be handed over to the holy people of the Most High. His kingdom will be an everlasting kingdom, and all rulers will worship and obey him. Daniel 7:27, NIV

This is Daniel's perspective about the prophetic future. The Church is waiting for the glorious day on which God will establish his Kingdom on earth. When He does so, he will remove all the other kingdoms and authorities. The Kingdom of God, his ruling, will remove all the kings who oppose Him.

Until that moment arrives, we, the Church, must understand that the Kingdom of God is here; but instead of introducing changes in the external and political order of things, it is spiritually working in people's lives with the purpose of establishing the lordship of Christ and make disciples of all cities and nations. As we will see in the next chapter it is accomplished as we begin to exercise influence over all areas of society better referred to as ***"the kingdoms of this world"***

We must seek the Kingdom of God above everything else, and the Lord will give us all things.

Our Father's good will is to give us the Kingdom.

Listen, dear friends. Isn't it clear by now that God operates quite differently? He chose the world's down-and-out as the kingdom's first citizens, with full rights and privileges. This kingdom is promised to anyone who loves God. James 2:5, The Message

Just as it was prophesied by Daniel, the Kingdom will come and all human sovereignty will be removed and substituted by God's sovereignty. The mystery, the new revelation is that this same Kingdom of God already came to work among men, but in an unexpected way. Not to destroy a human government or to abolish sin, but to work in the spiritual realm, in silence, in secret, without being revealed. However, the Lord's glory, his supernatural power will be revealed at the end of this age; this time not in silence but with great power and glory removing all sin and evil on earth.

> *But throughout the history of these kingdoms, the God of heaven will be building a kingdom that will never be destroyed, nor will this kingdom ever fall under the domination of another. In the end it will crush the other kingdoms and finish them off and come through it all standing strong and eternal. Daniel 2:44, The Message*

> *Then the end will come, when he hands over the kingdom to God the Father after he has destroyed all dominion, authority and power. For he must reign until he has put all his enemies under his feet. 1 Corinthians 15:24-25, NIV*

> *Christ, however, offered one sacrifice for sins, an offering that is effective forever, and then he sat down at the right side of God. There he now waits until God puts his enemies as a footstool under his feet. Hebrews 10:12-13, Good News Translation* (emphasis added by the author)

This is what the Gospel of the Kingdom is about: the future is invading the present.

> *What I'm trying to do here is get you to relax, not be so preoccupied with getting so you can respond to God's giving. People who don't know God and the way he works fuss over these things, but you know both God and how he works. Steep yourself in God-reality, God-initiative, and God-provisions. You'll find all your everyday human concerns will be met. Don't be afraid of missing out. You're my dearest friends! The Father wants to give you the very kingdom itself. Luke 12:29-32, The Message*

The Lord has given us the Earth; we must transform and disciple the nations until we have fulfilled our calling: to restore the "government" of God over his creation just as we were commanded in Genesis 1:28.

CHAPTER

14

THE
TRANSFORMATION
OF THE KINGDOMS
OF THIS WORLD

*Again, the devil took Him up on an
exceedingly high mountain, and
showed Him all the kingdoms of the world
and their glory. And he said to Him: "All
these things I will give You if You will fall
down and worship me"*

Matthew 4:8-9

*Then the seventh angel sounded: And there were
loud voices in heaven, saying: "The kingdoms of
this world have become the kingdoms of our Lord
and of His Christ, and He shall reign forever and
ever!" Revelation 11:15*

AGENTS OF CHANGE

At the beginning of Jesus' ministry, Matthew describes the temptation by the devil who offered the Lord the kingdoms of this world and their glory (fame, reputation, riches, honor, recognition, respect, etc.). John writes about the fulfillment of the command of the great commission and the calling of the Church to establish the ruling and lordship of Christ here on earth.

What must happen for us to be able to see the wonderful fulfillment of our calling? A transformation of the kingdoms of this world, where the government goes from Satan's control to Christ's lordship.

The 20th century saw the restoration of God's power of the Holy Spirit in the Church (EKKLESIA), this caused the greatest numerical explosion and growth since the day of Pentecost.

Every Christian is called to be an agent of change and an instrument of transformation; to share the good news of the gospel and to reveal the glory of God.

In the 21st century the Lord is preparing His EKKLESIA, for the most significative movement of discipling nations through a Church that understands the fullness of the great commission mandate with a Kingdom emphasis.

Psalm 2 is a Messianic Psalm that contains a surprising declaration that the Kingdoms of this world will come under the government of the son through His Church.

Ask of me, and I shall give thee the heathen for thine inheritance, and the uttermost parts of the earth for thy possession.[1]

The Bible states that Jesus is the creator of all things, That, all things created are for him and that we are joint heirs with him. We have been called to redeem the systems of influence of the nations.

It is well-known that "every" society and "every" culture has at least eight important areas of influence, and the body of Christ is called to try and intentionally make an impact on them so that the Kingdom will be able to advance. These areas are frequently referred as kingdoms or worlds in an interchangeable form.

The word *kingdom* is often referred to as a sphere of influence or the realm of influence. We can use the expression: the kingdom of sports or the world of sports, the animal or mineral kingdom, the world of music, the entertainment world, the political realm, etc. Following are the most significant areas of influence today:

- Family (the institution of family).
- Church (religion or lack of it).
- Commerce and the business world.
- Arts, entertainment and sports.
- Science and technology. (Including the Medical field)
- Education (schools, colleges and universities).
- Mass media of communication (radio, press and TV).
- Government and politics. (Including the Military)

1   *The King James Version*, (Cambridge: Cambridge) 1769.

In my opinion these are the kingdoms of this world offered to Jesus by the devil. I believe these are the gates of hell that Jesus told Peter would NOT prevail against His Church. Paul wrote: *Wherein in time past ye walked according to the course of this **world**, according to the prince of the power of the air, the spirit that now works in the children of disobedience. Ephesians 2.2.* John refers to them in 1 John 5.19: *And we know that we are of God, and the whole world lies in wickedness.*

The **first Biblical** reference to the word EKKLESIA, translated as Church is found in Mathew16.18 where Jesus states:

*And I say also unto thee, That thou art Peter, and upon this rock **I will build my church; and the gates of hell shall not prevail against it.** [19]And I will give unto thee the keys of the kingdom of heaven: and whatsoever thou shall bind on earth shall be bound in heaven: and whatsoever thou shall loose on earth shall be loosed in heaven. (Emphasis by the author).* Here, Jesus declares that there will be a conflict between His Church and the Gates of the kingdom of darkness.

The word *ekklesia* in the Greek language was used as an *assembly*. A place where the Greek citizens gathered to make decisions and to determine policies, to elect public leaders, it was a place where the business affairs of the city and local government where handled.

Proverbs 8.15 declares our calling to reign and to govern:

By me kings reign, and princes decree justice. [16]By me princes rule, and nobles, even all the judges of the earth. [17]I love them that love me; and those that seek me early shall find me. Revelation states that Jesus is the King of kings and the Lord of lords. The term *kings,* refers to those that govern in the kingdom. That we have been made Kings and Priests unto Him.

Genesis 22.17 states that the descendants of our father Abraham *will possess the gates of his enemies.*

Many Christians have preached the gospel of salvation and tried to make disciples of all nations bringing people to their congregations, but they have not seen their cities and nations being transformed. Jesus preached the gospel of the Kingdom trained and empowered his disciples and they began to turn the world upside down with a drastic cultural transformation.

In the Bible, mounts usually represent the authority of the kingdoms of this world. We must learn and teach how to occupy these kingdoms described before and bring the influence of heaven into the earth, transforming culture and influencing the nations until we are able to put his enemies under his feet. [2]

Some years ago I heard the renowned lecturer and writer John Maxwell define "leadership" as "influence". If we look at the influence that the Church has had on culture and society as a whole, we may deduce that in fact the changes are not many because the influence has been little due to our ignorance.

Understanding the dimension to which God is sending his Church in this day and age, is the first step to extend the Kingdom of God in the non-Christian world.

The Church is not the place where we meet; it is made up of every Christian who is well-trained and capable of being an influence in the world he lives and moves in.

2   M. Maiden. Turn the World Upside Down, Destiny Image Pub. 2011.

The five ministries empower believers for the work of their calling as agents of change and instruments of transformation, but it is the born-again men and women within the Church who must be a testimony of Christ to every person in their world of influence. Our mission is to make disciples of all nations, transform lives, fill and transform every area of influence in the culture and society which has been under the control of the non-Christian world spirit in the past.

GO INTO ALL THE WORLD...

Jesus left us this commission: *"Go into all the world and preach the gospel to every creature"*. Very often, the term *world* is understood as the political nations of the Earth; but in general this refers to the world we live and move in.

The Bible says in Acts 17:6: *These who have turned the world upside down have come here too*. Although it is a negative comment, I would add: "These are who transform the whole world". The meaning of the phrase *to turn upside down* is "to alter the regular order of something; to change the course or direction of something". We have the calling to turn the financial, political and educational systems upside down, all the world. The aim is that where the Church is present, the place can be transformed.

It is not necessary to be a pastor to transform or turn the world upside down, and to extend the Kingdom of God. We only need to obey and fulfill the calling that God has given us so that at the same time He is able to fulfill his purpose in our lives in this generation.

Every believer is called to preach the gospel. The word *preacher* does not mean someone who stands behind a pulpit or in the street to declare what the Bible says.

*The best way to preach is through our lifestyle
shown to the world of influence.*

Someone once said: "The priest preaches but he doesn't live it"; I think many Christians do a lot of talking but they are ineffective and their lives are not an example to be followed. They do not experience what they say or share. I prefer the expression: "He who lives well, preaches well".

Today, there are churches which have their Sunday service; on Monday, their prayer meeting, on Tuesday, their evangelism meeting, on Wednesday, their discipleship meeting, on Thursday, their cell groups, on Friday, their youth and women's meetings, on Saturday, their men's meeting... and again the Sunday service which stops them from fulfilling their calling to the unconverted world.

SHINING IN THE DARKNESS

When we accept Jesus as our Savior, we leave the world to come into the Church on a full-time basis. The Church has a well-defined purpose in order to be able to work properly in the world, but the problem arises when we shut ourselves up or take refuge in it and stop shining in the world day after day. There comes a time when we are surrounded only by *Christian* things: friends, entertainment, sports, parties, jobs, schools. We live in a Christian world with little or no influence at all on those who are not believers. We are not being light for them.

> *You are the light of the world. A city that is set on a hill cannot be hidden. Nor do they light a lamp and put it under a basket, but on a lampstand, and <u>it gives light to all who are in the house.</u> Matthew 5:14-15* (emphasis added by the author).

The city is the Church, the hill are the areas or kingdoms of this world.

We are the light that makes darkness disappear in the world where God has put us.

In the fourth century, St Augustine wrote the book *The City of God,* considered by many as the most influential book in history, with the exception of the Bible; it was a challenging tool for many of the men who had a big impact on the entire world, among them Charlemagne and John Calvin. They, and many others, tried to establish the Kingdom of God by applying the Christian principles, not only within the Church but also in the areas of culture, education, arts, industry and the political government. St Augustine's view consisted in an influential Church breaking through in every area of society.

Throughout recent history, there have been men and women of God who had a radical impact on the world in every area of society. Some of them were: Leonardo da Vinci, Copernicus, Galileo, Isaac Newton and Louis Pasteur in science; Johann Sebastian Bach, George Frederic Handel and Ludwig van Beethoven in music; John Calvin in education; Christopher Columbus, Joan of Arc, King James, John Wycliffe, Martin Luther... and the list goes on.

It is time to see the world through Jesus' eyes: a harvest field, a dark place in need of light. We should see our world as the missionary field to which God is sending us to transform it through our influence. We are called to be agents of change and instruments of transformation; to share the good news of the gospel and reveal his glory.

The field is the world, the good seeds are the sons of the kingdom (Matthew 13:38). Jesus was sent into the world and declared: *As long as I am in the world, I am the light of the world (John 9:5).*

In John 17:18 we find Jesus Christ's priestly prayer: *As You sent Me into the world, I also have sent them into the world.* John 17:15 says: *I do not pray that You should take them out of the world, but that You should keep them from the evil one.*

TO TRANSFORM OR NOT TO TRANSFORM… THAT IS THE QUESTION

A shadow over the present Church is the wrong interpretation of the second coming of Christ. We now believe that it is not worth making an effort because Jesus is returning soon. Due to this extreme thought buried deep in our minds, we have let the devil do his job in our society through the areas of influence. We must plan our lives as if Jesus were coming in 1,000 years' time and live them as if he were coming in five minutes.

The Church has taught that Jesus will come back to take us out of this world, when his prayer was: *I do not pray that You should take them out of the world, <u>but</u> that You should keep them from the evil one* (emphasis added by the author).

When the Church has a vision of Kingdom, not for its own gain but to influence politics, governments, the business world, arts, science, education, families and the Church itself, then the kingdoms of this world will be transformed to reach the fulfillment of Revelation 11:15: *The kingdoms of this world have become the kingdoms of our Lord and of His Christ, and He shall reign forever and ever!*

Nowadays what the Church needs most is to find men and women who are trained and ready to change the course of every nation. People who are determined to pay the price that God requires of them.

We must train a generation of "new wineskins", ready to receive the new wine from God.

The early Church invaded cities and transformed every area of society.

Tertullian, the great African Christian author, mocked the Roman Empire in these words: *We (the Church) are but of yesterday, and we have filled every place among you —cities, islands, fortresses, towns, markets, camps, tribes, companies, palace, senate, forum— we have left nothing to you but the temples of your gods.*[3]

According to Acts 3:21, the fulfillment of all times will be the "restoration of all things" God spoke about, when the Church has put all the enemies of Jesus Christ under his feet. The main subject in the Bible is the victory of the Kingdom of God over the kingdom of darkness: the final and irrevocable victory of Christ and his Church over the kingdoms of this world and their rulers of darkness.

Without a proper understanding of the future, we will not be able to plan for it or prepare the coming generations for the task at hand, this is why we must have a clear understanding of *the future and glorious calling of the Church.*

---

3   Mark Galli, Tertullian: Container of faith, Christian Reader 39, #1 (January/February 2001); J. Mattera, Ruling in the Gates, Creation House, 2001. P. 53.

Chapter 15

THE AUTHORITY OF THE KINGDOM

• • • *That the God of our Lord Jesus Christ, the Father of glory, may give to you the spirit of wisdom and revelation in the knowledge of Him, the eyes of your understanding being enlightened; that you may know what is the hope of His calling, what are the riches of the glory of His inheritance in the saints, and what is the exceeding greatness of His power toward us who believe, according to the working of His mighty power which He worked in Christ when He raised Him from the dead and seated Him at His right hand in the heavenly places, far above all principality and power and might and dominion, and every name that is named, not only in this age but also in that which is to come. And He put all things under His feet, and gave Him to behead over all things to the church, which is His body, the fullness of Him who fills all in all.* –Ephesians 1:17-23

AUTHORITY OVER ALL CREATION

Here Apostle Paul challenges the Church to know and receive the revelation of its wonderful future and the glory of its inheritance. And immediately after that, he describes *his mighty power.* The same power that raised Christ from the dead and seated Him at the right hand of the Father, with authority over "all" the visible and invisible creation for all eternity, putting all things under his feet.

The apostle also says that the Father of glory used this power, which is the Holy Spirit of God, to place his Church in a position of similar authority over all things; and describes that glorious Church taking part in the fullness of Christ and in a position over the Lord's creation.

Far from the dispensationalist theory, which does not match what the Bible says, God has determined a destiny of glory for his Church. From the biblical point of view, a power described as "mighty" cannot possibly be so ineffective that it needs to be rescued by God in order to avoid a period of suffering at the hands of a created being, whatever it may be. In fact, as we have already explained, affliction, tribulation and persecution are just a part of the process but the final destiny is a Church that will reign for all eternity.

The Church is the frame of God's ruling; it was designed by the Lord with a divine and eternal purpose.

Its purpose is to establish the Kingdom of God and his lordship, in all ages. In the Church we find the *pledoma,* the wholeness, the "fullnes" of everything that Christ is. The XXI century

Church, just like the Church in the book of Acts, is called and ready to be renewed, radical, restoring and reforming.

Prophets Haggai and Isaiah declared the glorious future of the Church at the end times. We can see that these prophecies have never had their fulfillment in the nation of Israel or the Jewish people. Therefore, we must understand them as words declared over the future of the spiritual Israel: the Church of the Lord.

> *For thus says the Lord of hosts: 'Once more (it is a little while) I will shake heaven and earth, the sea and dry land; and I will shake all nations, and they shall come to the Desire of All Nations, and I will fill this temple with glory,' says the Lord of hosts. 'The silver is Mine, and the gold isMine,' says the Lord of hosts. 'The glory of this latter temple shall be greater than the former,' says the Lord of hosts. 'And in this place I will give peace,' says the Lord of hosts. Haggai 2:6-9*

> *Arise, shine; for your light has come! And the glory of the Lord is risen upon you. For behold, the darkness shall cover the earth, and deep darkness the people; but the Lord will arise over you, and His glory will be seen upon you. The Gentiles shall come to your light, and kings to the brightness of your rising. Isaiah 60: 1-3*

The word translated as "glory" in these texts is *chabod* (Strong's #3519) which means: honor, splendor, power, authority, magnificence, riches, fame, dignity. The Lord declares that all this will be the future of "his Church".

CONQUERING THROUGH LOVE AND SERVICE

Today's leaders must train the Church members with a new pattern in their hearts, minds and spirits for the calling to establish the glory and magnificence of the Kingdom, the lordship and the ruling of Christ in our cities and nations. This will be our preparation to rule in the New Earth.

The Church must have a vision of conquest through love and service, exactly the same way you win the love and respect of your wife and children. If we long to see what we have never seen before, we will have to do what we have never done so far.

The Church needs a loving and service spirit together with the correct teaching about the new man and the new covenant that is able to renew our understanding.

We go from the gospel of salvation to a higher level: the gospel of the Kingdom. We go from Christ on the cross to the Christ seated on His heavenly throne.

The Church's message must change from condemnation, defeat or hopelessness, to victory and dominion; it is not a message of legalism or of the law, but of grace and forgiveness; it is not a message of sin, but of Christ's unconditional love.

The Church must have a dynamic teaching and be a people of conquest; those who have the courage to possess their inheritance.

The apostolic Church in the end times has the task of teaching an optimistic and triumphant eschatology where an Antichrist does not and will not reign, but where Christ reigns with his Church alongside. God is not preparing us for tribulation but for reigning and He wants us to have a mentality of ambassadors who are *"more than conquerors"*.

The apostolic Church lives and expresses the authority and the establishment of the Kingdom. It is a Church like the one in Ephesus that "grows and prevails".

The XXI century Church will grow and be developed in obedience, through the power of the Holy Spirit. The Lord will raise apostolic and prophetic teams in every nation to train the generation that will fulfill the commission of the Church.

In the present reformation, we are starting to see more and more Christian leaders in every area of influence in society. There are many Christian presidents, as it has been the case in Guatemala, Fiji, Uganda and other nations. And we will also see new Christian leaders in politics, business, education, science, arts, technology and the mass media of communication. We will soon witness more and more Christian corporations and companies making an impact in the commercial world; and Christian mass media of communication making an impact on unbelievers. Christian news will not appear only in the religious section of newspapers, but they will also cover frontpages. *¡The Kingdom of God* is approaching with power!

God is raising a generation of new wineskins, new times, new challenges, new experiences, new and wonderdul promises. A new generation that will open doors and prepare the way for its coming appearance.

God is trying to find just one thing: men and women of faith who are able to embrace a vision of tranformation and Kingdom.

THE RESTORED APOSTOLIC VISION

The Lord is restoring the Church in the last days to the lost truths, the anointing and the apostolic vision of the early Church from the very beginning. We can reach our eternal purpose because Christ paid the price demanded by God due to man's fall.

> *... and to make all see what is the fellowship of the mystery, which from the beginning of the ages has been hidden in God who created all things through Jesus Christ; to the intent that now the manifold wisdom of God might be made known by the church to the principalities and powers in the heavenly places, according to the eternal purpose which He accomplished in Christ Jesus our Lord, in whom we have boldness and access with confidence through faith in Him. Ephesians 3:9-12*

Until we have not embraced his vision, God will not give us his anointing. First, He gives us the vision, next He pours out his anointing and then He sends his provision. If there is no vision, there is no provision.

This vision includes the following:

- Territorial vision (vision of Kingdom).

- Fatherly spirit (to give life, disciple and send; to be a father).

- Spirit of warfare (intercession, prayer, spiritual warfare).

- A heart of unity (unity of conviction not of convenience).

- A heart to reach the nations.

- A heart for the afflictions of the people (to see things in God's eyes).

- Generational vision (to leave a generational inheritance; to be reproduced and multiplied).

- Vision of transformation for cities, regions and nations.

- Vision of dominion and lordship through the influence of love and service.